The Sources of WTO Law and their Interpretation

ELGAR INTERNATIONAL ECONOMIC LAW

Series Editors: Alan O. Sykes, *Frank and Bernice J. Greenberg Professor of Law, University of Chicago Law School, USA*

This monograph series is intended to provide a point of convergence for high quality, original work on various aspects of international economic and WTO law, ranging from established subject matter, such as international agricultural trade or the application of core trade disciplines such as MFN, to cross-cutting issues involving the interaction of international standards in the fields of investment, tax, competition, food safety and consumer protection with international trade law or the relationship of horizontal exceptions such as the general exception to domestic regulatory barriers. Theoretically rigorous, these books will take an analytical and discursive approach to the field, wherever possible drawing on insights from disciplines other than law, such as economics and politics, in an attempt to arrive at a genuinely inter-disciplinary perspective. Proposals are encouraged that primarily engage with new and previously under-developed themes in the field, or alternatively offer an innovative analysis of areas of uncertainty in the existing law.

Bringing together work from both established authors – academics and practitioners alike – and from a new generation of scholars, the Elgar International Economic Law series aims to play an important role in the development of thinking in the field.

Titles in the series include:

Reconciling Trade and Climate
How the WTO Can Help Address Climate Change
Tracey Epps and Andrew Green

International Economic Law and Monetary Measures
Limitations to States' Sovereignty and Dispute Settlement
Annamaria Viterbo

Accession to the World Trade Organization
A Legal Analysis
Dylan Geraets

Judicial Engagement of International Economic Courts and Tribunals
Michelle Q. Zang

The Law and Economics of WTO Law
A Comparison with EU Competition Law's 'More Economic Approach'
Marios C. Iacovides

The Sources of WTO Law and their Interpretation
Is the New OK, OK?
Petros C. Mavroidis

The Sources of WTO Law and their Interpretation
Is the New OK, OK?

Petros C. Mavroidis

Edwin B. Parker Professor of Foreign and Comparative Law, Columbia Law School, USA

ELGAR INTERNATIONAL ECONOMIC LAW

Edward Elgar
PUBLISHING

Cheltenham, UK • Northampton, MA, USA

Published by
Edward Elgar Publishing Limited
The Lypiatts
15 Lansdown Road
Cheltenham
Glos GL50 2JA
UK

Edward Elgar Publishing, Inc.
William Pratt House
9 Dewey Court
Northampton
Massachusetts 01060
USA

Paperback edition 2023

A catalogue record for this book
is available from the British Library

Library of Congress Control Number: 2022932832

This book is available electronically in the **Elgar**online
Law subject collection
http://dx.doi.org/10.4337/9781803921723

ISBN 978 1 80392 171 6 (cased)
ISBN 978 1 80392 172 3 (eBook)
ISBN 978 1 0353 1893 3 (paperback)

Printed and bound by CPI Group (UK) Ltd, Croydon, CR0 4YY

Contents

Acknowledgments

My interest in the study of sources of law originates in a collaboration in the 1990s with my friend and mentor, David Palmeter. We co-authored a piece on this score a few years ago, and the question of identifying and interpreting the WTO law has stayed with me ever since. Numerous subsequent discussions on this topic with Claus-Dieter Ehlermann, another good friend and mentor, helped me improve my thinking. And the more I have been thinking about it, the more I come to realize how important it is to adequately describe practice, since this is an area where, by construction, trade adjudicators enjoy substantial discretion. It is the manner in which discretion has been exercised that matters at the end of the day. In this short volume, I have attempted to present the manner in which discretion has been exercised, and critically evaluate the exercise of discretion in this respect, while framing it in a context that will incite, hopefully, additional work in this area.

As always, I had to rely on another old friend and mentor, Bill Davey, with whom I have discussed many of the issues in this book. Bill has been a tremendous inspiration in my work and, overall, in my approach to dispute adjudication. The same goes for Henrik Horn, with whom I have been thinking and writing about dispute settlement for almost 30 years.

Brad McDonald graciously offered his views whenever I tormented him with queries. I am most indebted to Eyal Benvenisti, Carlo-Maria Cantore, Adeet Dobhal, Kabir Duggal, Doug Nelson and Sunayana Sasmal, who provided me with detailed, critical comments on previous drafts that have greatly improved the coherence of my study. I have discussed a number of points in this study with Giovanni Distefano, Bernard M. Hoekman, Niall Meagher, André Sapir, Vassilios "Tzeve" Tzevelekos and Alan O. Sykes, and am grateful for their input. At Edward Elgar Publishing, Luke Adams, Vic Froggett and Helen Kitto have been magnificent throughout the process.

This book is dedicated to Claus-Dieter Ehlermann and David Palmeter, for all that they have done for me and many others like me, over the years.

Petros C. Mavroidis
New York City, December 2021

Abbreviations

ACP	African, Caribbean, Pacific
ADA	Anti-dumping Agreement
ADP	Anti-dumping Practices
BCI	Business Confidential Information
CITES	Convention on the International Trade of Endangered Species
CRS	Congressional Research Service
DSB	Dispute Settlement Body
DSU	Dispute Settlement Understanding
EU	European Union
FTA	Free Trade Area
GATT	General Agreement on Tariffs and Trade
GPA	Government Procurement Agreement
HS	Harmonized System
HSBI	Highly-Sensitive Business Information
ICJ	International Court of Justice
ICSID	International Centre for Settlement of Investment Disputes
ILC	International Law Commission
IMF	International Monetary Fund
ITU	International Telecommunications Union
LAN	Local Area Network
MAS	Mutually Agreed Solution
MEA	Multilateral Environmental Agreement
MFN	Most Favored Nation
MOU	Memorandum of Understanding
OECD	Organisation for Economic Co-operation and Development
PCIJ	Permanent Court of International Justice
POI	Period of Investigation

RBP	Restrictive Business Practice
SCM	Subsidies and Countervailing Measures
SPS	Sanitary and Phyto-Sanitary Measures
TBT	Technical Barriers to Trade
TDM	Trade Defense Mechanism
TRIPs	Trade-Related Intellectual Property Rights
TRP	Telecoms Reference Paper
USDOC	United States Department of Commerce
VCLT	Vienna Convention on the Law of Treaties
WCO	World Customs Organization
WIPO	World Intellectual Property Organization
WTO	World Trade Organization

Introduction to *The Sources of WTO Law and their Interpretation*

The commonplace view about the General Agreement on Tariffs and Trade (GATT) was that, for the most part, it was practically a self-contained regime, living in isolation from the rest of international law. This view was anchored on sound empirics, as GATT panels, especially in the early years of the GATT era, consistently interpreted the GATT by focusing on the text, and occasionally on the negotiating record. This picture changed, but only slightly so, during the later years of the GATT, following the establishment of the GATT Legal Office, and the increasing influence that trained jurists have had in the shaping of the GATT jurisprudence.

The advent of the World Trade Organization (WTO) signaled, among other things, a more conciliatory attitude towards international law, through the formal acknowledgment of recourse to customary rules of interpretation (codified in the Vienna Convention on the Law of Treaties or VCLT) as the statutory means to clarify the various obligations assumed under the WTO, which constitute the WTO sources of law. It is the framers of the WTO that introduced in Article 3.2 of the DSU (Dispute Settlement Understanding), the agreement administering adjudication in the WTO, a provision obliging panels to interpret the covered agreements through recourse to the customary rules of interpretation. It is WTO adjudicating bodies which understood this reference to mean recourse to the rules embedded in the VCLT, an international treaty that codifies customary international law in this realm.

While the identification thus of sources of law is the exclusive privilege of the WTO framers, the manner in which they will be interpreted is entrusted to the adjudicators.

The VCLT exhibits a double function:

- On the one hand, it allows the judge to identify interpretative elements of the WTO sources of law (the obligations assumed by adhering to the contract);
- On the other hand, following the identification of interpretative elements, the adjudicator will be asked to provide a taxonomy, a classification of each identified element under the various headings of the VCLT. The negotiating record of the GATT thus could come under Article 32 of the VCLT,

whereas a bilateral agreement between the disputing parties concluded at the negotiating stage could be, for example, part of the historical context.

Problems may arise in practice, as the VCLT is an incomplete contract, which invites judicial discretion regarding both the identification, as well as the classification of interpretative elements. How much of non-WTO law, for example, will be used to interpret assumed obligations, and what its intensity and legal significance will be, becomes, to an extent, a matter of discretion for WTO adjudicators. The exercise of discretion has important consequences: WTO panels have consistently held that, whereas some elements must anyway and under all circumstances be taken into account (those coming under the purview of Article 31 of the VCLT), others (those coming under the purview of Article 32 of the VCLT) will be employed, only if and when the adjudicator deems it warranted.

Practice reveals both inconsistencies ("noisy" judgments), as well as errors (false positives and negatives), both with respect to the extensive margin (which elements should be taken into account), as well as the intensive margin (their classification under the VCLT). The WTO adjudicator of course is hardly in an enviable position as it is called to interpret one incomplete contract (the WTO) through another incomplete contract (the VCLT). Furthermore, because of the discretion embedded in the VCLT, efforts to "complete" ex ante the WTO contract (of more than dubious efficacy, anyway) will unavoidably leave room for discretion, as it is impossible to undo the VCLT without risking putting into question its status as customary international law.

Some insurance policy is necessary in order to safeguard the role of the WTO adjudicator as an agent with a limited mandate who should not be behaving as law-maker. The fine line between sources of law and their interpretative elements should not, in other words, be trespassed. The VCLT was probably thought of as the insurance policy to this effect.

There are not quick and fast solutions. As feasible contracts remain obligationally incomplete, there will be need for a judge to "complete" it without trespassing the principal–agent mandate embedded in Article 3.2 of the DSU. Judges have no better tool than the VCLT when it comes to interpreting an international contract like the WTO. The question is: what is the skillset that WTO judges should possess, and how to ensure that only those possessing that skillset will get the nod to sit on the bench, and honor this exacting mandate. To some extent, the current WTO crisis is a crisis of the judiciary. With the Appellate Body currently in abeyance, this is probably the time to reflect on whether the VCLT has served its intended function or not.

1. What are sources of law and why do they matter?

1. DISTINGUISHING BETWEEN SOURCES OF LAW AND THEIR INTERPRETATIVE ELEMENTS

Pound (1946) identifies five different ways to define "sources of law" depending on the criterion used. He ends up privileging, for the purposes of his study which explores the interaction between the US legislative and judiciary, the following understanding of the term (p. 249): "we may well call the sources of law, answering the question how and by whom the content of legal precepts has been worked out, whence they got their content as distinguished from their force and authority ...".[1]

This is roughly the compass for our study as well. We will understand the term "sources of law" as legalese for the body of law governing relations among parties to a(n) (international) contract (agreement), like the WTO that we focus on in this study. "What are the sources of law?" is akin to asking "which law governs" the relationship between WTO members.

It is the contracting parties (the WTO members) that have the power to identify the law that will govern their relations in the contract that they adhere to, subject to constraints of public order that must be observed anyway. In the realm of international law, members of the international community must anyway observe *jus cogens* ("compelling law") from which no deviation is allowed for the members of the international community.[2] They must further observe customary international law whenever appropriate. These two sources of law are largely irrelevant for the purposes of WTO law, as the better arguments lie with the view that there is no international customary trade law to

---

[1] Roscoe Pound. 1946. Sources and Forms of Law, Notre Dame Lawyer, A Quarterly Law Review, XXI: 247–314. Fuller (1969), in a similar vein, asks "where does the judge obtain the rules by which to decide cases?", p. 69 in Lon Fuller. 1969. The Anatomy of Law, Praeger Publishing: New York City, New York.
[2] See the compelling short account of Alfred Verdross. 1966. Jus Dispositivum and Jus Cogens in International Law, American Journal of International Law, 60: 55–63.

start with. Already Jackson (1969) had persuasively claimed that even MFN (most favored nation), the foundational discipline in the GATT, had not acquired the status of customary international law.[3] Subsequent practices of WTO members when transacting with non-members have left no one in doubt that Jackson's claim was, and continues to be, legitimate.

We are left with the contractual arrangement, the balance of rights and obligations that the membership has agreed upon. Alas, for various reasons, the expression of the agreed package is not always self-interpreting, and disputes arise. And this is where the fun begins. As things stand, it is impossible to forecast when and where disputes will arise in equilibrium. What is clear to one signatory might be unclear to another.

Disputes can of course arise not only for good faith, but for bad faith reasons as well, and this is the quintessential reason why it is difficult (or impossible) to forecast when disputes will arise. Judges will be asked in either case (good faith or bad faith) to provide the information necessary to adjudicate disputes. In Pound's (1946) and many others' accounts, a judge will find (identify) the legal precept (canon), interpret it, and apply it to the facts of the case.

International trade agreements do not necessarily include provisions on dispute adjudication. Koremenos (2007), in her empirical study, showed that the majority of the earlier free trade areas (FTAs) made no provision for dispute adjudication whatsoever.[4] More recently, this trend has been reversed, and is now definitely leaning towards including dispute adjudication (in similar arrangements). The overall volume of litigation before FTAs though still remains scarce.[5] As we do not observe forum diversion with respect to adjudication of trade disputes, WTO bodies continue to be the forum for adjudication par excellence. The process before them is what we will be discussing in the following pages.

The WTO includes its own adjudication regime, the DSU. WTO members are the principals, and sign an agency contract with the adjudicators, their agents.[6] Through this contract, they instruct their agents to apply a certain body of law when adjudicating their disputes. Consequently, the principals

---

[3]   John H. Jackson. 1969. World Trade and the Law of the GATT, Bobbs-Merrill: Indianapolis, Indiana.

[4]   Barbara Koremenos. 2007. If Only Half of International Agreements Have Dispute Resolution Provisions, Which Half Needs Explaining? Journal of Legal Studies, 36: 189–211.

[5]   Aaditya Mattoo, Nadia Rocha and Michele Ruta (eds.). 2020. Handbook of Deep Trade Agreements, The World Bank Group: Washington, D.C.

[6]   It is a bit more complicated than that. The DSU tasks the WTO Secretariat with the role of assisting panels (Article 27), and with decisive powers in the selection of panelists. In case parties cannot agree, it is the Secretariat that will, upon request, compose the Panel (Article 8.7). We discuss all this in more detail in section 7.1.

do not only determine the sources of law, but also the ambit of their disputes. As a result, finding the applicable law in a given dispute is no open season. If WTO adjudicators take the view that the law invoked is ill-suited to deal with the factual claim submitted, then they can only reject the complaint. What they definitely cannot do is replace the submitted claim with their preferred legal basis and continue to adjudicate. The subject matter of disputes is circumscribed by the disputing parties with respect to both the factual matter as well as the legal issues involved, and no one else.

WTO courts are not courts of general jurisdiction. They do not have the power to judge *ex aequo et bono* ("from equity and conscience") like the International Court of Justice (ICJ), which possesses powers to this effect, and can rule on any issue of international law (WTO law included).[7] WTO courts have a narrower mandate, as they must address the requests submitted within the four corners of the (WTO) law identified by the parties, or simply reject the request, as we have already suggested.

Assuming that the complainant has put forward the correct legal basis, the WTO adjudicator's agreement to this effect is tantamount to finding the source of law that will appropriately serve as the basis to adjudicate the dispute. But this is only the first step, as the adjudicator will be called to interpret the legal basis identified in the complaint. Because the WTO contract requests for WTO adjudicators to resolve disputes by employing the customary rules of interpretation, WTO adjudicators must follow the pathway established by these rules. This pathway allows judges to identify interpretative elements that they will use in illuminating the content of the sources of law, and eventually in applying the outcome of their interpretative exercise to the facts of the case.[8]

Thirlway (2019),[9] when discussing sources of law in international adjudication, claims that law is, at the end of the day, what courts say it is. This might sound like an exaggeration, but assuming the (international) community has

---

[7]   As we discuss later, though, a WTO member that submits a WTO dispute to the ICJ violates Article 23 of the DSU.

[8]   Even though relevant to this study, there is not much point in delving into the details of the Hart-Dworkin debate regarding the extent of discretion that courts enjoy. Instead, we will discuss the record from an empirical perspective, by asking what law WTO adjudicators have applied when resolving submitted disputes. The views of Dworkin on legal positivism have been exposed in Ronald Dworkin. 1977. Taking Rights Seriously, Harvard University Press: Cambridge, Massachusetts, where he criticized H.L.A. Hart. 1961. The Concept of Law, Oxford University Press: Oxford, United Kingdom.

[9]   Hugh Thirlway. 2019. The Sources of International Law, 2nd edition, Oxford University Press: Oxford, United Kingdom. Fuller (1969) mentions a series of legal theorists and even conservative judges, like Charles Evans Hughes of the US Supreme Court, associating themselves with this view (pp. 23 et seq.). The latter is quoted by the

subscribed to peaceful adjudication of disputes, and since disputes routinely arise, the word of the adjudicators is often the last word on the state of law. For it is law as understood in case law that will ultimately decide a dispute. The interest thus, in researching the sources of law as practiced by WTO courts, is in that it is only through this inquiry that we can have the full picture of the law governing the relations between the 164 trading nations participating in the WTO.

2.   A PRESENTATION OF THE VOLUME

The rest of the volume is divided into six chapters, and in Chapter 8, the ultimate chapter, we recap the main conclusions of this study.

Chapters 2, 3, and 4 reflect a presentation of the relevant legal framework, that is the WTO sources of law, as established in the WTO contract. We kick off in Chapter 2 with a discussion of the sources of law as understood in the WTO contract itself. We will show that the WTO contract does not address head-on this issue in detailed manner, other than through a reference to the "covered agreements". In this vein, we will distinguish between "primary law", that is, the various agreements coming under the aegis of the WTO, which we discuss in Chapter 3, and "secondary law", that is instances where the contract empowers WTO bodies to legislate, which we discuss in Chapter 4. Chapter 4 thus includes a presentation of sources of law that WTO bodies explicitly mentioned in the WTO contract itself are empowered by legislative fiat to adopt.

Chapter 5 deals with custom and general principles of law. None of them qualify as a source of law, hence their treatment in a separate chapter. Case law, with one exception, has closed the door to the relevance of custom as a source of substantive obligations assumed by the whole of the membership. The same case law has opened the door to general principles of law, which it has used, for all practical purposes, as supplementary means of interpretation (that is, not as independent sources of law).

In Chapter 6, we shift gears and move on to discuss the various interpretative elements of the WTO sources of law. This is where we will be delving into the workings of the VCLT: the instrument that WTO adjudicators have used to interpret the various provisions since the very first dispute that was submitted to them. We will first show that, through the use of the VCLT, WTO courts have identified various interpretative elements, and have also provided their taxonomy, thus varying their legal relevance in WTO law. We will also inquire

---

same author, stating: "We are under the Constitution, but the Constitution is what the judges say it is" (p. 24).

into the nature of the agency contract that the WTO members have signed with their adjudicators, and explore the consequences (actual and potential) of the arrangement. It is in this chapter that we will argue that there is only so much that principals can do to "tame" the discretion of WTO adjudicators, and provide thus a basis for the claim that the identity of adjudicators matters.

Chapter 7 consists of a critical assessment of practice. It is in a way the empirical counterpart to the more doctrinal Chapter 6. There are three key takeaways from the discussion in this chapter. First, WTO adjudicators have largely resolved disputes using (almost) exclusively the covered agreements as sources of law. They have only occasionally had recourse to non-WTO law, and when doing so, solely for the purpose of confirming an interpretation that they had already reached. Second, case law has not been internally coherent and consistent. The establishment of the Appellate Body, one might have thought, could have proven to be a catalyst that would reap gains from innovation by picking the correct panel approach, and crystallizing it into de facto precedent that subsequent panels would follow. Alas, the Appellate Body has not risen to this challenge. Third, the problem has been exacerbated partly because WTO adjudicators have not shied away from their duties. They have never pronounced *non liquet* (literally translated as "it is not clear"), and sent the ball back to the legislators' camp. Their attitude had been largely condoned until recently when the Trump Administration pulled the rug out from under the WTO dispute settlement edifice.

Chapter 8 recaps briefly the main conclusions of the study, and then explains why "noisy" judgments (variations across inter-WTO adjudicators), with respect to the understanding and interpretation of sources of law, matter. In this chapter, we will argue that there is no magic bullet. We are miles away from solving problems with this. Perhaps the size of the problem, though, could be reduced through additional "completion" of the WTO contract, crystallization of case law, and a more rigorous process for selecting WTO adjudicators, especially at the panel level.

2. The statutory definition of WTO sources of law

1.   THE SOURCES OF WTO LAW

The DSU does not mimic other regimes that explicitly and specifically circumscribe the sources of law that the courts established should use. It does provide guidance to this effect, even if in an oblique and not comprehensive, head-on manner, and thus provides some guidance for WTO adjudicators to implement. The cursory treatment of such an important issue in the DSU has ignited debates in literature, where academics vie for hard-to-reconcile positions. The epicenter of academic disputes has to do with the question of whether, and if so how much, non-WTO law can be appropriately referred to when adjudicating disputes between WTO members originating in the WTO contract. A look into practice is warranted, under the circumstances.

1.1.   The Incomplete Treatment of Sources of Law in the DSU

Article 38 of the ICJ Statute reads:

1. The Court, whose function is to decide in accordance with international law such disputes as are submitted to it, shall apply:
   a. international conventions, whether general or particular, establishing rules expressly recognized by the contesting states;
   b. international custom, as evidence of a general practice accepted as law;
   c. the general principles of law recognized by civilized nations;
   d. subject to the provisions of Article 59, judicial decisions and the teachings of the most highly qualified publicists of the various nations, as subsidiary means for the determination of rules of law.
2. This provision shall not prejudice the power of the Court to decide a case *ex aequo et bono*, if the parties agree thereto.

The DSU does not read like this at all. It does not contain a provision specifying one by one the sources of law that WTO courts can use in order to resolve disputes that might arise between WTO members, not even one of indicative nature. Various statutory provisions though establish that respondents can only raise claims of violation of a "covered agreement", that is, one of the agreements coming under the aegis of the WTO. Article 1 reads:

> 1. The rules and procedures of this Understanding shall apply to disputes brought pursuant to the consultation and dispute settlement provisions of the agreements listed in Appendix 1 to this Understanding (referred to in this Understanding as the "*covered agreements*"). (emphasis added)

Article 3.2 of the DSU states: "Recommendations and rulings of the DSB cannot add to or diminish the rights and obligations provided in the *covered agreements*" (emphasis added). Article 4.3 of the DSU, in similar vein, underscores that: "If a request for consultations is made pursuant to a *covered agreement* ..." (emphasis added). Finally, Article 7 of the DSU reads:

> 1. Panels shall have the following terms of reference unless the parties to the dispute agree otherwise within 20 days from the establishment of the panel:
> "To examine, in the light of the relevant provisions in (name of the *covered agreement*(s) cited by the parties to the dispute), the matter referred to the DSB by (name of party) in document ... and to make such findings as will assist the DSB in making the recommendations or in giving the rulings provided for in that/those agreement(s)."
> 2. Panels shall address the relevant provisions in any *covered agreement* or agreements cited by the parties to the dispute. (emphasis added)

A straight-forward textual reading of all these provisions, accordingly, should lead to the conclusion that the mandate of WTO adjudicators is limited to the scope of the "covered agreements". WTO panels are not courts of general jurisdiction. And yet, a controversial WTO panel report (Korea-Procurement, which we discuss in Chapter 5), and discussion regarding what all these provisions do *not* exclude, have ignited disputes across academics regarding the delineation of WTO sources of law.

1.2. Why Practice Matters

In academic literature, the question has arisen whether WTO courts could still have recourse to all public international law from which the DSU has not explicitly contracted out. This issue has been a bone of contention between Pauwelyn and Trachtman. Pauwelyn (2003)[1] sees WTO law as part and parcel of wider public international law which, in principle, applies to WTO disputes

---

[1]   Joost Pauwelyn. 2003. Conflict of Norms in Public International Law, Oxford University Press: Oxford, United Kingdom; Joel Trachtman. 2004. Conflict of Norms in Public International Law: How WTO Law Relates to Other Rules of International Law, American Journal of International Law, 98: 855–902; and Joel Trachtman. 1999.

unless the WTO has explicitly contracted out, and Trachtman (1999) and (2004) argues the opposite case. In Trachtman's view, public international law applies to the extent there is some legislative authority explicitly embedded in the DSU to this effect; there can be no recourse to it by default.

Trachtman's argument is based on the statutory language used in the DSU, which is the expression of legislative will. Case law has overwhelmingly sided with Trachtman, even though there is one report (Korea-Procurement), which we discuss later on, which echoes Pauwelyn's view. Empirical accounts looking into all case law since the inception of the WTO, like Cook (2015) and Mavroidis (2008),[2] have confirmed that Trachtman's view has prevailed in practice, and we will be providing evidence to this effect in Chapters 3, 4, and 5.

This nevertheless does not mean that non-WTO law cannot be used as interpretative element for the WTO sources law. It can and it has been used as such, and in the same chapters we will be looking into relevant practice on this score. And, of course, there is a fine line in practice sometimes between a source of law and an interpretative element. Depending on the weight that the interpreter, for example, accords to "a relevant rule of international law" in interpreting a provision of a covered agreement, non-WTO law can on occasion exert dramatic influence on the understanding of case law. Still, we lack observations to this effect, as WTO adjudicators have consistently used non-WTO law to confirm interpretations reached by analyzing the text of a provision.

1.3.   A Taxonomy of WTO Sources of Law

For the purposes of this study, we divide the sources of WTO law into primary and secondary law. Primary law refers, as expected, to the sources of law embedded in the covered agreements. What is left then? What could possibly come under our suggested term "secondary law"? What could it cover?[3] To respond to this question, we need to take a closer look into the institutional architecture of the WTO contract.

The Domain of WTO Dispute Resolution, Harvard International Law Journal, 40: 333–80.

[2]   Graham Cook. 2015. A Digest of WTO Jurisprudence on Public International Law Concepts and Principles, Cambridge University Press: Cambridge, United Kingdom; Petros C. Mavroidis. 2008. No Outsourcing of Law? WTO Law as Practiced by WTO Courts, American Journal of International Law, 102: 421–74.

[3]   Wolfgang Benedek is the first to have used the term "secondary law" to describe a series of consensus-based decisions by the GATT contracting parties, see Wolfgang Benedek. 1990. Das GATT aus Völkerrechtlicher Sicht, Springer Verlag: Heidelberg.

The covered agreements themselves establish a series of WTO organs (bodies), and provide them with the legal capacity to create law. Article IX of the Agreement Establishing the WTO, for example, states that the WTO members can, through joint action, adopt interpretations of the existing legal framework. Article X of the same Agreement provides that members can, through joint action, adopt amendments of the WTO Agreement. Indeed, the road to adopting the first ever WTO amendment has been opened, following a decision by the WTO General Council to amend Article 31 TRIPs. The power to adopt interpretations or amendments is conferred, by virtue of these provisions, to the highest organs established, the WTO Ministerial Council and General Council.

Various lower in hierarchy WTO bodies, the "WTO Committees", such as the Committee on Antidumping Practices (ADP Committee) or the Technical Barriers to Trade (TBT) Committee, meet and adopt decisions and recommendations that could be of general applicability, and their legal effects have been recognized in WTO jurisprudence. The first two paragraphs of Article 13 of the TBT Agreement, for example, circumscribe the powers of the TBT Committee in the following manner:

13.1 A Committee on Technical Barriers to Trade is hereby established, and shall be composed of representatives from each of the Members. The Committee shall elect its own Chairman and shall meet as necessary, but no less than once a year, for the purpose of affording Members the opportunity of consulting on *any matters* relating to the operation of this Agreement or the furtherance of its objectives, and shall carry out such responsibilities as assigned to it under this Agreement or by the Members.

13.2 The Committee shall establish working parties or other bodies as may be appropriate, which shall *carry out such responsibilities as may be assigned to them by the Committee* in accordance with the relevant provisions of this Agreement. (emphasis added)

The wording of the cited provision is certainly wide enough to allow for law-making at the level of the TBT Committee. The same is true for various other committees. We will return to this discussion in Chapter 4, where we provide some empirical proof that law-making has indeed happened in similar bodies.

We thus use the term "secondary law" to refer to the output by WTO bodies that appears in the covered agreements.

3. The WTO primary law

1. PRIMARY LAW

Following our definition of "primary law" in the previous chapter, in what follows we distinguish between the agreements appearing in Appendix 1 (entitled "Agreements Covered by the Understanding"), and agreements incorporated in the covered agreements.

1.1. The Covered Agreements

Appendix 1 to the DSU includes an exhaustive list of all covered agreements, namely:

(A) Agreement Establishing the World Trade Organization
(B) Multilateral Trade Agreements
     Annex 1A: Multilateral Agreements on Trade in Goods
     Annex 1B: General Agreement on Trade in Services
     Annex 1C: Agreement on Trade-Related Aspects of Intellectual Property Rights
     Annex 2: Understanding on Rules and Procedures Governing the Settlement of Disputes
(C) Plurilateral Trade Agreements
     Annex 4:[1]
          Agreement on Trade in Civil Aircraft
          Agreement on Government Procurement
          International Dairy Agreement
          International Bovine Meat Agreement
There should be no doubt that these agreements constitute sources of WTO law, as this is precisely what the term "covered agreements" appearing, for example, in Article 1.1 of DSU amounts to. If a member has breached an obli-

---

[1] Annex 4 Agreements (plurilaterals) have been negotiated by a sub-set of the WTO membership, and bind only the signatories. To add a new agreement, the membership has to consent.

gation assumed under these agreements, a dispute can be lawfully submitted before the WTO adjudicator.

1.2. Agreements Incorporated by Reference

Various covered agreements incorporate other international agreements, which thus (by fiat of incorporation), become a source of WTO law themselves as well. Several problems can arise though, as incorporated agreements might have been interpreted before courts in the past, or continue to be interpreted in a forum other than the DSU. This raises the question of the relevance of similar interpretations in WTO law, which we tackle in what follows.

Before doing that, we should note that WTO agreements can and have been interpreted by a forum other than the WTO panels. But WTO members cannot submit disputes arising under the WTO contract anywhere else but to a WTO panel. Article 23.2 DSU pertinently reads to this effect:

> ... Members shall:
> (a)   not make a determination to the effect that a violation has occurred, that benefits have been nullified or impaired or that the attainment of any objective of the covered agreements has been impeded, *except through recourse to dispute settlement in accordance with the rules and procedures of this Understanding*, and shall make any such determination consistent with the findings contained in the panel or Appellate Body report adopted by the DSB or an arbitration award rendered under this Understanding ... (emphasis added)

Consequently, a WTO panel can lawfully neglect and/or set aside an interpretation of WTO law by a non-WTO forum, leaning on the above cited provision. The same, however, is not necessarily true when incorporated agreements are part and parcel of a different regime, which includes its own adjudication procedures. A look thus into WTO practice regarding this issue becomes necessary, in order to discern the attitude of WTO adjudicators in this respect.

1.2.1.   The GATT
The GATT 1994,[2] one of the Annex 1A agreements,[3] consists of the GATT, which has been incorporated as such with no amendment, and a series of

---

[2]   The name "GATT 1994" was privileged to denote that, in the WTO era, not only the original text of the GATT ("GATT 1947") but also its amendments, protocols of accession, protocols of certification, etc., would be a covered agreement.

[3]   The Agreement Establishing the WTO, the foundational charter for organizing multilateral trade, has three Annexes (agreements) comprising substantive obligations: 1A, trade in goods; 1B, trade in services; 1C, trade-related intellectual property rights.

other documents (protocols of certification, protocols of accession, etc.) that were adopted by the GATT members over the years during the pre-WTO era (1948–94). Whereas the overwhelming majority of instruments added to the original GATT are discernible, there is one element, embedded in Article 1(b)(iv) of GATT, which is far from being self-interpreting. This provision makes it clear that, besides identifiable legal instruments, GATT 1994 also includes: "... *other* decisions of the CONTRACTING PARTIES to GATT 1947" (emphasis added).

What does the term "other decisions" mean? It is quite likely that the framers, fearing that an exhaustive enumeration of instruments might have led to unwarranted omissions ("type 2 errors", or false negatives), wanted to grant adjudicators (eventually) latitude and discretion to identify the legal instruments that should be considered an integral part of GATT 1994. A simple perusal of the covered agreements suffices to persuade the reader that the WTO framers were quite keen to keep the links to GATT practice tight. Recall that Article XVI:1 of the WTO Agreement reads:

> Except as otherwise provided under this Agreement or the Multilateral Trade Agreements, the WTO shall be guided by the decisions, procedures and customary practices followed by the CONTRACTING PARTIES to GATT 1947 and the bodies established in the framework of GATT 1947.

In practice, the question arose of whether the term "other decisions" covered panel reports as well. Unlike practice in the WTO era, during the GATT years, panel reports would not be adopted at the mere request of the winning party. Panel reports were adopted by consensus. These reports thus enjoyed a veneer of legitimacy. Furthermore, some other reports were never adopted, and their legal relevance was therefore questionable.

The question of whether adopted GATT panel reports qualify as "other decisions" arose in Japan—Alcoholic Beverages II. The panel responded in the affirmative (§6.10). The Appellate Body disagreed. In its view, adopted reports were an important part of the "GATT acquis" (p. 15), a term that it invented, and not detailed any further. The issue arose again in the panel report on US—FSC. The panel held that decisions to adopt reports should come under Article XVI of the Agreement Establishing the WTO. The Appellate Body agreed, albeit in a roundabout way (§115):

> We recognize that, as "decisions" within the meaning of Article XVI:1 of the *WTO Agreement*, the adopted panel reports in the *Tax Legislation Cases*, together with the 1981 Council action, could provide "guidance" to the WTO. The United States believes that the "guidance" to be drawn from the 1981 Council action, through footnote 59, is that the FSC measure is not an "export subsidy". The present dispute involves the interpretation and application of Article 3.1(a) of the *SCM Agreement*

and the question of whether the FSC measure involves export subsidies *under that provision*. In contrast, the 1981 Council action addresses the interpretation and application of Article XVI:4 of the GATT 1947. The "guidance" that the 1981 Council action might provide, therefore, depends, in part, on the relationship between these different provisions. (emphasis in the original)

What does guidance actually mean? It is definitely less than precedent, but how much less? Is there an obligation to consider it, or do panels have total discretion to this effect? At the end of the first sentence in the above quoted paragraph, the Appellate Body use the term "could", most likely to denote that there was no obligation to refer to past case law, never mind adhere to it.

In practice, WTO panels have routinely had recourse to adopted GATT panel reports in order to confirm an interpretation reached through other elements of the VCLT. A very representative instance is the panel report on Korea—Commercial Vessels, where the panel used the findings of a GATT panel when interpreting the term "serious prejudice" (§§7.591–602).

But even unadopted GATT panel reports can be usefully referred to, even though the Panel on Japan—Alcoholic Beverages II held that they (§6.10): "have no legal status in either the GATT or the WTO system since they have not been endorsed through decisions by the Contracting Parties to GATT or WTO Members".

The panel on US—Lamb looked at both adopted and un-adopted GATT reports to support one of its findings (§7.78), as did the panel on EC—Pipe Fittings (§7.280). Practice reveals that panels retain discretion to do so, when they find the analysis in unadopted reports persuasive. So much for the term "other decisions".

The GATT 1947 (which is an integral part of GATT 1994) incorporates the Havana Charter, so we are, in this respect, in the presence of "double incorporation".[4] Article XXIX of GATT embeds a best-endeavor to observe Chapter V of the Havana Charter, which regulates restrictive business practices (RBPs). The panel on Mexico—Telecoms used Article 46 of the Havana Charter to inform its understanding of the term "anti-competitive practice" (§7.236). In so doing, the panel made it clear that it was using the relevant provision of the Havana Charter as a "supplementary means of interpretation" of an obligation assumed under a covered agreement (the GATS, General Agreement on Trade in Services), and not as a source of law applicable in adjudication.[5]

---

[4]   The GATT 1947 also explicitly refers to the Articles of Agreement of the International Monetary Fund (IMF), which we discuss separately below.

[5]   Before this report, one could have plausibly argued that Article XXIX GATT had fallen into desuetude. This provision required from WTO Members to observe certain chapters of the Havana Charter, pending the acceptance of the latter and the establish-

1.2.2. Agreements incorporated in the TRIPs Agreement

The TRIPs (Trade-Related Intellectual Property Rights) Agreement mentions in Article 1.3 major international conventions dealing with the protection of intellectual property, namely, the Paris Convention (1967), the Berne Convention (1971), the Rome Convention, and the Treaty on Intellectual Property in Respect of Integrated Circuits. Specific provisions of the TRIPs Agreement require observance of various provisions of these agreements like, for example, Article 9 of TRIPs, which requires WTO Members to comply with Articles 1–21 of the Berne Convention.

The panel on US—Section 110(5) Copyright Act discussed the legal relevance of secondary law under the incorporated agreements. The agreement (Berne Convention) authorizes a special rapporteur to make express mention of the possibility available in some national legislations of entering "minor exceptions", a term appearing in Articles 11(1) and 11bis(1) of the Berne Convention. Though not inserted as an amendment to the Convention, the rapporteur's report was adopted by the contracting parties, and this fact sufficed for the WTO Panel to consider the report as a "subsequent agreement" between the parties (to the Berne Convention and not the WTO) in accordance with Article 31.2(a) of VCLT, which reads:

> 2. The context for the purpose of the interpretation of a treaty shall comprise, in addition to the text, including its preamble and annexes:
>   (a) any agreement relating to the treaty which was made between all the parties in connexion with the conclusion of the treaty; (§6.53)

To confirm that its understanding of the term "minor exceptions" was correct, the panel examined state practice in this realm that had occurred even after the conclusion of the TRIPs agreement (§6.55).

WTO panels have acknowledged the legal significance of the preparatory work of the incorporated agreements as well: the panel on Canada—

---

ment of the International Trade Organization (ITO). The ITO never came into being, and the advent of the WTO on January 1, 1995, signaled the definitive end to the ITO saga. In the 1960s and 1970s, many of the countries that had acceded to the GATT had no domestic competition law and were engaging, as is widely reported in the literature, in restrictive business practices, thus violating the letter and the spirit of Chapter V of the Havana Charter, one of the chapters that they were supposedly expected to observe by virtue of Article XXIX GATT. Since no complaint has ever been filed alleging a violation of this provision, even though there are various WTO members that have not even enacted competition laws, the available evidence suggests that in WTO state practice, the provision was legally inoperative. Then came the WTO panel on Mexico—Telecoms. Note though, that the Appellate Body has never pronounced on the continued relevance of Article XXIX.

Pharmaceutical Patents took into account the preparatory work of the Berne Convention to confirm the interpretation it had reached about provisions of the TRIPs agreement (§7.70).

Thus, in the realm of agreements incorporated in the TRIPs agreement, panels have opened the door towards acknowledging the legal significance of secondary law as well. Secondary law though, like amendments to an incorporated agreement, can occur even after the WTO has entered into force. This was not the case in the dispute discussed above. But this was precisely the case in the context of an OECD (Organisation for Economic Co-operation and Development) arrangement, which formed the subject matter of a dispute under the SCM (Subsidies and Countervailing Measures) Agreement. We turn to this issue next.

1.2.3. Agreements incorporated in the SCM Agreement

The WTO Agreement on Subsidies and Countervailing Measures (SCM) provides in its Annex I(k) that:

> [I]f a Member is a party to an international undertaking on official export credits to which at least twelve original Members to this Agreement are parties as of 1 January 1979 (or a successor undertaking which has been adopted by those original Members), or if in practice a Member applies the interest rates provisions of the relevant undertaking, an export credit practice which is in conformity with those provisions shall not be considered an export subsidy prohibited by this Agreement.

It did not take long to have a dispute concerning the understanding of this provision, and case law has left no one in doubt that the "international undertaking" mentioned is the Arrangement on Guidelines for Officially Supported Export Credits (Arrangement on Guidelines) of the OECD. But only a sub-set of the WTO members are OECD members, so should they be acknowledged the right to amend a WTO source of law? Or should, conversely, the WTO membership at large have to abide by the original OECD text, whereas WTO members who are also OECD members should observe any subsequent amendment as well?

In Brazil—Aircraft (Article 21.5—Second Recourse), the panel faced, inter alia, precisely this question: is the OECD arrangement of 1998 (the amendment to the arrangement incorporated in the SCM Agreement), which had been negotiated only among OECD members, that is, among only a small minority of WTO members, binding on the WTO Membership? The panel decided that, because of the reference in item (k) to a "successor undertaking", it also had to take into account the 1998 arrangement. The WTO membership thus had, by including these words, outsourced legislative activity on a sub-set of the SCM Agreement to the OECD. This means that a small minority of the WTO membership can add to and/or amend the existing sources of WTO law in this particular field, namely, export credits.[6]

1.2.4.   The International Monetary Fund (IMF)
Article XV.4 of GATT 1947 reads:

> Contracting parties shall not, by exchange action, frustrate* the intent of the provisions of this Agreement, nor, by trade action, the intent of the provisions of the Articles of Agreement of the International Monetary Fund.

Consequently, by acceding to the GATT, WTO members, irrespective of whether they are IMF members or not,[7] should at least avoid frustrating the intent of the IMF Articles of Agreement, which thus become a source of law that panels must take into account.

In fact, with respect to problems concerning monetary reserves, balances of payments, or foreign exchange arrangements (Article XV.2), and assuming a dispute has been raised, panels must consult with the IMF and accept its determinations in this context (Appellate Body report on Argentina—Textiles Footwear §§84–85). Exchange controls and restrictions can be used, but only in accordance with the Articles of Agreement of the IMF (Article XV.9), and, in case of dispute, panels must have recourse to this body of law to ensure that the respondent has acted lawfully (panel report on Dominican Republic— Import and Sale of Cigarettes §§7.139–142). So, in this respect as well, WTO members have ceded space to the IMF.

The relationship between the WTO legal order and the IMF is further elaborated in an inter-organizational agreement that the respective Heads of the WTO and the IMF have signed. We will turn to it later on, as at this point, we conclude our discussion on the scope of WTO primary law.

---

[6]   The panel on Argentina—Financial Services referred extensively to OECD documents as supplementary means of interpretation, even though the GATS does not include references to the OECD (§§7.509 et seq.).

[7]   Not all WTO members are IMF members as well. Cuba and Taiwan are not IMF members.

4. The WTO secondary law

1. SECONDARY LAW

Recall, the term "secondary law" does not appear as such in the Agreement Establishing the WTO. We "invented" it to denote all WTO law that has been created after the advent of the WTO by the WTO competent bodies. The competence to legislate originates always in the Agreement Establishing the WTO, and in this chapter we refer to secondary law created by WTO bodies, and not by extra-WTO bodies (like the OECD and the IMF), which we have discussed in the previous chapter.

Recall, the principals, the WTO members themselves, acknowledged the right to adopt legal acts in various provisions of the Agreement Establishing the WTO. In this vein, the WTO members can adopt interpretations (Article IX.2), amendments (Article X), and can even grant waivers to WTO members, allowing them thus to "exit" provisionally from their contractual obligations (Article IX.3). Finally, by virtue of Article VIII, the WTO possesses legal personality, and can transact under its name. It has already signed a headquarters agreement with the Swiss Confederation, and has concluded agreements with the IMF and the World Bank.

The membership has established various bodies which, under the Agreement Establishing the WTO, have the right to adopt decisions to this effect. By virtue of Article IV.1 for example, the Ministerial Conference, the highest WTO body, can adopt decisions on all matters concerning the covered agreements. But since it meets only every two years, it is the WTO General Council that effectively assumes responsibility for the day-to-day operations, as well as the various Councils (Article IV.5), their subsidiary bodies (Articles IV.6), and the committees mentioned in Article IV.7.

With this in mind, we turn to a discussion of the various legislative initiatives that WTO bodies are empowered to perform.

1.1. Interpretations

The WTO Membership can, by virtue of Article IX.2 of the Agreement Establishing the WTO, adopt interpretations of any provision included in the covered agreement by a three-fourths majority (if no consensus was possible).

This provision embeds a specific process: it is upon recommendation by the Council that the Ministerial Conference will adopt an interpretation.

In US—Clove Cigarettes, the Appellate Body held that paragraph 5.2 of the Doha Ministerial Decision (which defined the term "reasonable interval" appearing in Article 2.12 of the TBT (Technical Barriers to Trade) Agreement to mean a period of at least six months) was not an interpretation in the sense of Article IX.2, because no recommendation by the Council had been issued before it was adopted (§§250 et seq.). It found instead that it constituted a "subsequent agreement" between the members in the sense of Article 31 VCLT (§§257 et seq.). This is a reasonable conclusion in light of the fact that the framers of the DSU had conditioned the adoption of interpretations upon the observation of a specific process.

An interpretation by the membership affects the balance of rights and obligations for the whole membership (Appellate Body report on US-FSC, footnote 127), and, when adopted, is added to the sources of WTO law. No interpretation has been adopted so far. The closest the world trading community came was with the enactment of the above quoted paragraph 5.2.

1.2.   Waivers

A waiver is a flexibility clause. To address an exceptional circumstance (that, arguably, cannot be effectively countered through recourse to any other means) a WTO member can request from the membership permission to disrespect its obligations ("waive" its duty to this effect). A waiver, besides the legal disciplines waived, imposes conditions that must be observed, and also provides for a maximum duration (which can be extended).[1] Waivers thus reduce the number of provisions that a WTO member must observe, but only following a decision by the membership to this effect.

Waivers are justiciable. In EC—Bananas III, both the panel and the Appellate Body considered the scope of the waiver to the European Union (EU). The EU and the African, Caribbean and Pacific (ACP) countries had signed the Lomé Convention, and argued before the Appellate Body that the panel should have deferred to the interpretation advanced by the EU and the ACP, who were the only ones competent to interpret it (§§7.95–97). The Appellate Body disagreed. In its view, the waiver itself was a WTO decision that, as such, could be reviewed by WTO adjudicating bodies (§169).

---

[1]   See for example, GATT Doc. W.9/228 of February 26, 1955, the waiver that the US was granted to deviate from its obligations under Articles II and XI of GATT, in order to help American farmers.

Waivers thus are a source of law as they include the obligations that (certain) WTO members do not have to observe (provisionally), and (often) the conditions allowing the agreed deviation.[2]

1.3. Amendments

Amendments are distinct from interpretations, as Article 3.9 of the DSU makes clear:

> The provisions of this Understanding are without prejudice to the rights of Members to seek authoritative interpretation of provisions of a covered agreement through decision-making under the WTO Agreement or a covered agreement which is a Plurilateral Trade Agreement.

Article IX.2 of the Agreement Establishment of the WTO, clarifies that "authoritative interpretations" and "amendments" are distinct instruments: "This paragraph shall not be used in a manner that would undermine the amendment provisions in Article X".

In EC—Bananas III, the Appellate Body underscored this point, when stating in §7.569:

> Such multilateral interpretations are meant to clarify the meaning of existing obligations, not to modify their content. Article IX.2 emphasizes that such interpretations "shall not be used in a manner that would undermine the amendment provisions in Article X".

But as we saw above, there is no exact definition of "authoritative interpretation" in the WTO legal arsenal. It seems fair to argue, though, that through authoritative interpretations, WTO members cannot undo the balance of rights and obligations. To do this, WTO members would have to amend the "covered agreements". Whereas through the adoption of an authoritative interpretation a clarification of ambiguous provisions is sought, through an amendment the content of a provision will be altered (as opposed to clarified). Amendments are discussed in Article X of the Agreement Establishing the WTO, and are adopted under different procedures from that followed when adopting authoritative interpretations.

On December 6, 2005, the WTO General Council opened the door for the adoption of the first (and, so far, only) amendment.[3] On January 23, 2017,

---

[2] WTO Doc. WT/GC/W/795 of December 18, 2019 includes all waivers granted to date.

[3] General Council Decision, Amendment of the TRIPS Agreement, WTO Doc. W T/L/641, of December 8, 2005. Through the new Article 31bis, WTO Members can outsource production of goods coming under compulsory licensing.

the Protocol Amending the TRIPs Agreement entered into force (for those who had already signed it), and since then, the General Council has extended the period for acceptance of the Protocol Amending the TRIPs Amendment several times, most recently until December 31, 2021 (for those who still wished to join in).[4]

On July 27, 2017, the General Council adopted a decision under Article X.8 of the Agreement Establishing the WTO to amend the Trade Policy Review Mechanism as of January 1, 2019, and to extend the periods for compiling country reports.[5]

1.4.   Agreements Signed by the WTO

The Agreement Establishing the WTO falls short of explicitly acknowledging a treaty-making power for the WTO, but a combination of various provisions achieves the same objective. Article VIII.1 acknowledges that the WTO has legal personality. Article V states that the WTO General Council can make arrangements that will facilitate the cooperation between the WTO and institutions having a related mandate. Finally, Article III.5 explicitly provides for cooperation between the WTO, the International Monetary Fund, and the World Bank.

The WTO has, in fact, signed international agreements. Besides its Headquarters Agreement which it signed with the host nation, the Swiss Confederation, the first two involved, as expected, the Bretton Woods institutions, the agreement between the International Monetary Fund and the WTO, and the agreement between the International Bank for Reconstruction and Development, the International Development Association, and the WTO.[6] These agreements, which were approved by the WTO General Council at its meeting on November 7, 8, and 13, 1996, were intended to strengthen the WTO's relationship with IMF and the World Bank. The WTO has concluded two more agreements: one with the WIPO (World Intellectual Property Organization)[7] and one with the World Organization for Animal Health (formerly the Office International des Epizooties).[8]

The relevance of such agreements has already been acknowledged in case law: the Appellate Body, in its report in Argentina—Textiles and Apparel, held

---

    [4]   WTO Doc. WT/L/1081 of December 11, 2019. The list of the WTO members who have already signed it is available at www.wto.org/english/tratop_e/trips_e/amendment_e.htm.

    [5]   WTO Doc. WT/L/1014 of July 27, 2017.

    [6]   General Council Decision, WTO Doc. WT/L/195, of November 18, 1996.

    [7]   35 ILM 754 (1996).

    [8]   WTO Doc. WT/L/272 of July 8, 1998.

that the agreement between the WTO and the IMF is legally relevant but that it does not modify, add to, or diminish the rights and obligations of Members (§72).

1.5.   Other Acts by WTO Bodies

The Agreement Establishing the WTO does not include an exhaustive list of all its organs. Indeed, as we have seen above, WTO committees have the authority to establish additional bodies, when warranted. But it is not only committees that have this right.

Article IV reflects the structure of the WTO, as well as the hierarchy across the bodies mentioned. Importantly in §6, it provides:

> The Council for Trade in Goods, the Council for Trade in Services and the Council for TRIPS *shall establish subsidiary bodies* as required. These subsidiary bodies shall establish their respective rules of procedure subject to the approval of their respective Councils. (emphasis added)

Even though "subsidiary bodies" have the power to decide issues, the legal significance of their output is not *ex ante* prejudged. In more general terms, the framers of the WTO seemed reluctant to add institutional detail in this respect. Lack of formalism permeates the foundational document, the Agreement Establishing the WTO, maybe because the framers, influenced by GATT's positive experience in this respect, consciously (and conspicuously) opted for a flexible regime that would address real challenges. Pragmatism was the hallmark of GATT, especially in its early years. But this was a different GATT. It was a GATT comprising a homogenous membership. It came very close to a textbook definition of a relational contract. The interminable negotiations and surrounding acrimony of the Tokyo Round should have been a wake-up call: the time for formalism had arrived. But probably, the fall of the Berlin wall and the ensuing (temporary?) apotheosis of liberalism persuaded the framers that the trading community was now on the same page. The leading nations might have thought that the WTO would continue to do business as usual, with the GATT's lack of formalism serving as compass. If at all, institutional detail would come in small doses, leaving ample room for discretion, and this is how the Agreement Establishing the WTO reads.[9]

---

[9]   We discuss all this in detail, in Petros C. Mavroidis. 2022. The WTO Dispute Settlement System, How, Why and Where? Edward Elgar Publishing: Northampton, Massachusetts and Cheltenham, United Kingdom.

To provide but two illustrations, which, in our view, do not suffer at all from sample bias, we will look into two provisions of the TBT, and the Anti-dumping Agreement.

Article 13.1 of the TBT Agreement explains the function of the TBT Committee:

> The Committee shall elect its own Chairman and shall meet as necessary, but no less than once a year, for the purpose of affording Members the opportunity of consulting on any matters relating to the operation of this Agreement or the furtherance of its objectives, and shall carry out such responsibilities as assigned to it under this Agreement or by the Members.

In similar vein, Article 16.1 of the Anti-dumping Agreement (ADA) reads:

> The Committee shall carry out responsibilities as assigned to it under this Agreement or by the Members and it shall afford Members the opportunity of consulting on any matters relating to the operation of the Agreement or the furtherance of its objectives. The WTO Secretariat shall act as the secretariat to the Committee.

Both committees meet regularly and are tasked to further the objectives of the respective agreements, but the legal significance of their output is nowhere prejudged, even though a substantial amount of the WTO "legislative" activity takes place within these subsidiary bodies, at the lowest level of the WTO institutional hierarchy. These bodies are usually staffed with technical experts, and not with political appointees, and they are thus better suited to entertain discussions on technical issues.[10] The Agreement Establishing the WTO does not specify the type of acts that WTO bodies can issue, nor their legal significance and/or hierarchy across different types.[11] Working procedures of various WTO committees refer to "decisions" and/or "recommendations", without however explaining what the difference is between the two. Rule 33 of the Working Procedures of the Committee on Anti-dumping Practices (ADP) reads: "where a decision cannot be arrived at by consensus, the matter at issue shall be referred to the Council for Trade in Goods".

Not every decision by each and every WTO organ is of regulatory character. But some are. The period of investigation (POI) during which a domestic investigating authority must establish dumping and measure injury is nowhere defined in the ADA. The ADP Committee filled the gap, as we discuss later on. What is the legal value of such acts?

---

[10] See the discussion regarding legislative activity at this level, in Andrew Lang and Joanne Scott. 2009. The Hidden World of WTO Governance, European Journal of International Law, 20: 575–614.

[11] There is one exception: Article IX.4 refers to a "decision" to grant a waiver.

In the absence of ex ante resolution, it was for WTO panels to decide this issue. Over the years, WTO adjudicating bodies have taken a friendlier attitude toward decisions and recommendations adopted by WTO organs. The panel on India—Quantitative Restrictions was one of the first to deal with this issue. It held that, if the committee (*in casu*, the Committee on Balance of Payments) had already decided an issue that was subsequently submitted to a panel, it could "see no reason to assume that the panel would not appropriately take those conclusions into account" (§§5.93–94). Indeed, this panel indicated that, depending on the treaty language and the legal powers conferred upon an organ such as the Balance of Payments Committee, it would potentially be legally compelled to do so.

Likewise, the panel on Mexico—Anti-dumping Measures on Rice relied (§7.62), in part, on the aforementioned ADP Committee recommendation on the length of the POI to support its own view as to the period over which to measure injury (injury POI). Along the same lines, the panel on EC—Pipe Fittings based its conclusion, that it is desirable that the period to investigate occurrences of dumping (dumping POI) substantially overlap with the injury POI, on the same recommendation (§7.321). The panel on Argentina—Poultry Anti-dumping Duties relied on the same document to support its conclusion that the dumping and injury POIs should not necessarily end at the same time (§7.287). The Panel on Guatemala—Cement II acknowledged that the recommendation reflected common practice (§8.266), whereas the Appellate Body in its report on Mexico—Anti-dumping Measures on Rice upheld a panel finding to the effect that, although non-binding, the recommendation on the length of POI could be usefully employed to support conclusions by the panel (§169).

Note that the panel on India—Quantitative Restrictions was dealing with a "decision" by a committee, whereas the other reports mentioned dealt with "recommendations". None of them paid inordinate attention to the qualification of the act it was dealing with, never mind drawing any consequences from it.

WTO adjudicating bodies have treated the ADP recommendation on POI as "supplementary means of interpretation". Is this classification inappropriate? It is true that a recommendation by the ADP Committee is not an interpretation in the sense of Article IX.2 of the Agreement Establishing the WTO: this provision acknowledges that only two WTO bodies, namely, the Ministerial Conference and the General Council, have the right to adopt interpretations. The same provision further requires the observance of a specific process that must be followed to this effect.

Article 16.1 of the Anti-dumping Agreement does not preclude the ADP Committee from exercising regulatory functions. Indeed, its mandate as specified in that article is quite open ended: it "shall carry out responsibilities as assigned to it under this Agreement or by the Members". In principle, nothing stops WTO members from delegating regulatory authority at this level. A recommendation like the one on the length of the POI could, conceivably, serve as a source of law. When adopting the recommendation on POI, the ADP Committee filled a legislative gap, as it dealt for the first time at the multilateral level with an issue not explicitly regulated in the AD Agreement, and the recommendation itself was accepted by consensus. Why then should not this act by the ADP Committee be accepted as interpretation (as per Article IX of the Agreement Establishing the WTO) instead?

A very strong counterargument can be made that ultimately justifies the choice of WTO adjudicating bodies to treat similar recommendations as supplementary means of interpretation, and not as sources of law. The General Council has a quorum provision: Rule 16 of its Working Procedures[12] specifically states that the majority of the WTO Membership must be present for a quorum. There is no quorum requirement for any of the committees established under the various covered agreements. This difference cannot be accidental. The will of the legislator must have been to associate the General Council meetings with a certain degree of formal significance, whereas the reverse is true for committee meetings. Would it then be legitimate to acknowledge "interpretation" status to acts by WTO committees, which could have been adopted when only an un-representative sample of the membership was present in the room?

By the same token, the expectation of trade delegates to the WTO must be that "serious" issues will be discussed at the General Council-level, whereas more day-to-day operations will form the subject matter of the committee mandates. Nothing stops the membership anyway from pushing a committee recommendation all the way to the higher echelons and couching it in the veneer of an "interpretation".

Note, finally, that one Panel has even reviewed the relevance of an act by a non-standing (that is, an ad hoc, a non-permanent) WTO organ, albeit as a supplementary means. In its determination that the term "anti-competitive practice" covered horizontal price fixing, the Panel on Mexico—Telecoms relied, in part, on the work of the "WTO Working Party on the Interaction of Trade and Competition Policies", which the Panel found to be of some relevance. The Panel treated the WTO Working Party report as a supplementary means of interpretation. This remains though, an isolated instance, and its relevance for future practice should not be exaggerated.

---

[12]   WTO Doc. WT/L/28, of February 7, 1996.

1.6. Panels, the Appellate Body, and the Role of Precedent

Working procedures of the WTO adjudicating bodies are discussed with a broad brush in statutory language, when it must have been clear to all that adjustments on a case-by-case basis would have proved necessary in practice. The DSU, of course, explicitly acknowledges the right of WTO courts to establish their own Working Procedures. Article 17.9 of the DSU, for example, explicitly refers to this right of the Appellate Body. The Appellate Body has indeed adopted its Working Procedures, which it applies across cases.[13] Panels are required to obey the Working Procedures reflected in Appendix 3 to the DSU, and Article 12.1 of the DSU permits them to deviate if they so choose. In practice, panels adopt working procedures on an ad hoc basis, for each dispute they litigate, adjusting the aggregate procedures (embedded in Appendix 3) to the particularities of the disputes that they are facing.

Like all feasible contracts, the Working Procedures are "incomplete", in that they do not contain all information that is necessary for WTO courts to perform the tasks assigned to them. For example, there is no discussion regarding the allocation of the burden of proof across litigating parties. Unless panels (and the Appellate Body) addressed this issue early on, they would have found it impossible to honor their mandate. What happened then in practice?

In US—Wool Shirts and Blouses, the Appellate Body invoked a legal maxim well-known in some orders, in order to allocate the burden of proof: *actori incumbit probatio* (the burden of proof weighs on the plaintiff). A few authors have argued that the Appellate Body was simply adding a veneer of legalese to consistent practice, as panels had always behaved in this way because they felt they had implied powers to this effect.[14] These powers originate in Article 11 of the DSU, which imposes a duty to make an "objective assessment", as well as in another legal maxim, in *praesumptio innocentiae* (presumption of innocence).[15] For, unless one is prepared to recognize that the duty to make an objective assessment includes powers to allocate the burden

---

[13] WTO Doc. WT/AB/WP/6 of August 16, 2010.

[14] Lorand Bartels. 2001. Applicable Law in WTO Dispute Settlement Proceedings, Journal of World Trade, 35: 499–519, was the first to make this point. See also Henrik Horn and Petros C. Mavroidis. 2009. Burden of Proof in Environmental Disputes in the WTO: Legal Aspects, European Energy and Environmental Law Review, 18: 112–40. Holmes (1991) might have classified it as an "interstitial characteristic of judicial lawmaking".

[15] Gabrielle Marceau. 2002. WTO Dispute Settlement and Human Rights, European Journal of International Law, 13: 753–814, advances a series of arguments in favor of this approach.

of proof, panels would have found it impossible to make an assessment (never mind an objective one) in the first place.

The DSU is equally silent with respect to the burden of persuasion. Whereas the term "burden of proof" asks the question "who should submit the proof?", the term "burden of persuasion" deals with the issue "how much proof is required for the party submitting it to prevail in litigation?" Article 3.8 of the DSU mentions that, in case an infringement of a provision has been demonstrated, there is *prima facie* evidence (sufficient to establish a fact or raise a presumption) that the rights of the party alleging as much have been nullified and/or impaired. Probably inspired by this language, in US—Wool Shirts and Blouses, the Appellate Body held that the party making a claim must make a *prima facie* case that its argument holds (§14).[16]

In subsequent cases, panels have understood the requirement "to make a *prima facie* case" as equivalent to raising a presumption that what is claimed is true (US—Stainless Steel, at §6.2). The panel in Mexico—Taxes on Soft Drinks ruled that the duty of the complainant to make a *prima facie* case is not affected by the defendant's decision not to challenge the claims and arguments made: Mexico had chosen not to raise any defense against some of the claims advanced by the US. The panel held that Mexico's inaction did not amount to admission that the US had made a *prima facie* case, and proceeded to establish whether this had been the case (§§8.16ff.).[17]

Consequently, while the allocation of the burden of proof is not explicitly addressed in the DSU, practice reveals that the WTO adjudicating bodies have made headway and produced a substantive body of law in this respect. The question of burden of persuasion, is (indirectly) prejudged only, in the realm of the Antidumping Agreement, where Article 17.6(ii) states:

> Where the panel finds that a relevant provision of the Agreement admits of *more than one permissible interpretation*, the panel shall find the authorities' measure to be in conformity with the Agreement if it rests upon one of those permissible interpretations. (emphasis added)

We will return to this provision later on when we discuss *non liquet* ("it is not clear"). For now, it suffices to state, that the burden of persuasion is not addressed anywhere else in the DSU.

---

[16]   "*Prima facie*" is of course, not a self-interpreting term. It seems akin to the common law standard of "preponderance of evidence", but it all depends on how it is exercised in practice. By adding to the evidence required to demonstrate a violation of the WTO in (most) SPS disputes, the WTO judge de facto reduced the potential for regulatory chill, while increasing the deterrence-factor vis-à-vis potential complainants, see on this score, Kaplow (2012).

[17]   In similar vein, see the panel report on US—Zeroing (Korea) at §§7.34ff.

To conclude our discussion, had WTO panels not addressed the twin questions of burden of production and burden of persuasion, they would not have been in a position to absolve their mandate. Under the circumstances, the term "implied powers" describes adequately that, in this context, panels have behaved like agents, and they have not acted contrary to Article 3.2 of DSU by claiming a power they do not possess in the first place.

Allocation of burden of proof and deciding on the burden of persuasion are necessary steps for panels to honor their objective function under Article 11 of the DSU: to make an objective assessment of the matter before them.

The treatment of confidential information is another area where panels have improvised. Article 8.3 of the SCM (Subsidies and Countervailing Measures) Agreement reads:

> A subsidy programme for which the provisions of paragraph 2 are invoked shall be notified in advance of its implementation to the Committee in accordance with the provisions of Part VII. Any such notification shall be sufficiently precise to enable other Members to evaluate the consistency of the programme with the conditions and criteria provided for in the relevant provisions of paragraph 2. Members shall also provide the Committee with yearly updates of such notifications, in particular by supplying information on global expenditure for each programme, and on any modification of the programme. Other Members shall have the right to request information about individual cases of subsidization under a notified programme.

Footnote 34 adds an important detail: "It is recognized that nothing in this notification provision requires the provision of confidential information, including confidential business information".

A few panels have adopted specific procedures for the submission of business confidential information (BCI). The panel on Korea—Commercial Vessels is an appropriate illustration, as it includes BCI procedures in its Attachment 2. In EC and Certain Member States—Large Civil Aircraft, the panel went one step further and adopted procedures for submission of Highly-Sensitive Business Information (HSBI) (Annex E to the panel report).

With these cases panels did not add a new right, but simply varied the degree of confidentiality in order to better protect the submission of confidential information, and thus facilitate the process, and honor their duty to make an objective assessment of the matter before them.

But panels have also introduced procedural innovations even when it was not necessary to do so in order to perform their tasks. A classic example is the so-called "enhanced third party rights".

Third parties are entitled to receive the first written submissions of the parties to a dispute made during the first meeting of the panel (Article 10.3 of DSU). They may also present their views at a session of the first substantive meeting of the panel (Appendix 3.6 to the DSU). The request for acknowledging "enhanced third party rights" arose first in EC—Bananas III, when a number of developing countries, which were appearing as third parties before the panel, requested that they be permitted to attend the second meeting with the panel as well (§7.4).[18] The panel, in light of the fact that the export revenue for a series of developing countries risked being heavily affected by the outcome of this dispute, agreed to the request, and allowed them to participate in the second meeting as well, (even though it denied them third parties' participation at the interim review stage, as explained in §§7.8 and 7.9 of the report).

In EC—Hormones, two separate panels were established, and were composed of the same individuals. The two panels were asked to examine identical measures that the EU had adopted and applied to the complainants. Each of the two complainants (Canada and the US), had reserved the right to participate as third party in the other panel. The two panels decided to give both Canada and the US access to all information submitted, and allowed them to participate in the second meeting as well (§8.15), and the Appellate Body upheld this decision (§154).

The panel on US—1916 Act (EC) (a dispute between the EU and the US) reflects a request by Japan, which was the complainant in parallel proceedings on the same issue, to be granted enhanced third party rights (§6.33). Japan cited the ruling of the EC—Hormones case to substantiate its request. The Panel denied the request, finding that particular circumstances existed in EC—Hormones that did not exist in the US—1916 Act cases (§6.35). On appeal, the Appellate Body affirmed the panel's approach, stating however (§150) that the panel's discretion was subject to appellate review.[19] The issue arose again in EC—Tariff Preferences. The panel issued a formal decision in this respect echoing the solution in EC—Bananas III because of the similarities across the two cases (Annex A, page A-2).

"Enhanced third party rights" is a panel innovation that by now has become a mainstay in WTO jurisprudence and practice. Have panels created a new procedural right through this case law? It seems to be the case indeed. The panel reports examined above did establish criteria which they referred to when deciding to accept or reject petitions in subsequent cases. And WTO members, as the above produced evidence underscores, have repeatedly requested enhanced third party rights.

Yet another innovation is the organization of open hearings. Article 14.1 of DSU reads: "Panel deliberations shall be confidential".

---

[18] In US—Large Civil Aircraft (Second Complaint), the panel held that it is for the party requesting enhanced rights to carry the associated burden of proof (§ 7.16).

[19] WTO Doc. WT/DS246/R, Annex A, Page A-1.

Still, although the above quoted provisions seem to be unambiguous, in a few cases so far, following a request to this effect, panels have agreed to organize hearings open to the public, adopting specific procedures to this effect. EC—Hormones is a very appropriate illustration to this effect.[20]

And we are not through with procedural innovations contributed by panels in WTO practice. Yet another example concerns the participation of *amici curiae*. Nothing in Appendix 3 (the legal instrument embedding the template for Working Procedures of panels) provides for participation of *amici curiae*. In US—Shrimp though, the Appellate Body criticized the panel's decision to reject an *amicus* brief. In a few paragraphs which only a trapeze artist or an expert in legerdemain could properly appreciate, the Appellate Body ended up concluding that the verb "to seek" appearing in Article 13 of the DSU does not exclude that panels should decline outright unsolicited information. First the Appellate Body underlined the following sentences in Article 13:

> Each panel shall have the right to seek information and technical advice from any individual or body which it deems appropriate.
> Panels may seek information from any relevant source ...

Then in §107, it held:

> If, in the exercise of its sound discretion in a particular case, a panel concludes inter alia that it could do so without "unduly delaying the panel process", it could grant permission to file a statement or a brief, subject to such conditions as it deems appropriate. The exercise of the panel's discretion could, of course, and perhaps should, include consultation with the parties to the dispute. In this kind of situation, for all practical and pertinent purposes, the distinction between "requested" and "non-requested" information vanishes. (emphasis added)

The Appellate Body invented a few conditions, included in the emphasized terms above, and addressed for the first time an issue that the framers had probably not even thought about when negotiating the DSU. What followed was mayhem. An extraordinary session of the Council was convened, and almost all WTO members criticized, if not excoriated altogether, the attitude of the Appellate Body.[21] Even though we still lack a comprehensive study on

---

[20] See   www.wto.org/english/tratop_e/dispu_e/public_hearing_sep06_e.htm. Ehring (2008) provides an account in this respect, see Lothar Ehring. 2008. Public Access to Dispute Settlement Hearings in the World Trade Organization, Journal of International Economic Law, 11: 1021–34.

[21] For a detailed review of the reactions, see Petros C. Mavroidis. 2002. Amicus Curiae Briefs Before the WTO: Much Ado About Nothing, pp. 317–29 in Armin von Bogdandy, Petros C. Mavroidis and Yves Meny (eds.). European Integration and

the impact of *amicus* briefs to the WTO,[22] existing studies point to lack of influence, and consistent overlooking of submitted briefs.[23]

One might wonder whether a hasty reaction aiming to ensure that the WTO highest court is tuned in to contemporaneity (instead of a politically legitimate solution adopted by the membership) demoted instead of promoted non-state actors from sensitizing WTO courts to their own concerns and worries. More on this later. What is clear is that a number of non-state actors, based on prior practice, have submitted their briefs to WTO courts over the years, implicitly adhering to the view that they have a (conditional) right to do so, even though the WTO sources of law make no room for similar submissions.

And there are other examples of similar procedural innovations by WTO panels. The Appellate Body has no remand authority. It cannot send a case back to the original panel and ask it to re-consider. The absence of remand is particularly problematic in cases where the original panel has exercised judicial economy. Assuming this has been the case, and the Appellate Body has also reversed the panel's findings, the complainant will have to re-introduce its claims to a new panel and start the process all over again.[24] To prevent this from being the case, the Appellate Body has employed a technique that it calls "completing the analysis".

In §§117–18 of its report in Australia—Salmon, the Appellate Body, regrouping all of its prior case law on the issue, went on to state that, when the factual record before it is sufficient, it will go ahead and complete the analysis. Thus, in US—Wheat Gluten, it reversed the causation analysis proposed

International Co-ordination, Studies in Trans-national Economic Law in Honour of Claus-Dieter Ehlermann, Kluwer: Leiden, the Netherlands.

[22]   Kearney and Merrill (2000) use various proxies in an attempt to "quantify" the impact of *amicus* briefs on the case law of the US Supreme Court, see Joseph D. Kearney and Thomas W. Merrill. 2000. The Influence of Amicus Curiae Briefs on the Supreme Court, University of Pennsylvania Law Review, 148: 743–98.

[23]   Charwat (2016) provides a comprehensive record of *amicus* submissions, whereas Ortino (2009) concludes that *amicus* briefs have had no influence on the shaping of WTO case law, see Nicola Charwat. 2016. Who Participates As Amicus Curiae in World Trade Organisation Dispute Settlement and Why? New Zealand Universities Law Review, 27: 337–64 (available at SSRN: https://ssrn.com/abstract=3021553); and Federico Ortino. 2009. The Impact of Amicus Curiae Briefs in the Settlement of Trade and Investment Disputes, pp. 301–16 in K. Meessen, M. Bungenber and A. Puttler (eds.). Economic Law as an Economic Good: its Rule Function and its Tool Function in the Competition of Systems, European Law Publishers: Munich, Germany.

[24]   On this issue, Palmeter (1998) on the one hand, and Busch and Pelc (2010) on the other have presented conflicting views, see N. David Palmeter. 1998. The WTO Appellate Body Needs Remand Authority, Journal of World Trade, 32: 41–4; Marc L. Busch and Krzysztof J. Pelc. 2010. The Politics of Judicial Economy at the World Trade Organization, International Organization, 64: 257–79.

by the panel, and then went on to complete the analysis based on the factual information before it (§§80 and 127). But in US—Carbon Steel, it declined to complete the analysis in light of the lack of clarity as to factual aspects of the case (§138).[25]

When deciding to complete the analysis, the Appellate Body ipso facto deprives WTO members of a two-instance adjudication. "Completing the analysis" is a procedural source of law that has been "invented" by WTO courts, and is unnecessary to resolve disputes.

But of the procedural innovations mentioned above, only the treatment of *amicus* briefs has been met with hostility by the membership. There is acquiescence with respect to both enhanced third-party rights,[26] as well as "completing the analysis". The former increases the participation (and possibly the influence) of the membership in litigation, whereas the latter contributes to speedy resolution of disputes. All members can profit. In fact, there was no critique against either expressed during the ongoing DSU Review.[27] But *amicus* briefs usually originate in specific quarters, and all do not profit the same. Probably, this is where the explanation for the membership's reactions lies. For the purposes of our chapter though, all three "innovations" should be understood as procedural rights, and thus sources of law. WTO practice shows that the membership has acquiesced to these two innovations that WTO courts have introduced.[28]

---

[25] See also the Appellate Body reports, Canada-Periodicals at pp. 21 et seq.; Canada—Autos, §133. Some case law is hard to reconcile even when applying the Appellate Body's criteria for completing the record. In EC—Asbestos, for example, the Appellate Body declined to complete the analysis even though the factual record before it sufficed by and large to do so, because in its view the GATT and the TBT (Technical Barriers to Trade) Agreement, are not part of a logical continuum, §§79–82. But in a subsequent case (US—Softwood Lumber IV), it returned to its prior approach, where the decision to complete the analysis hinges only on the adequacy of the factual record (§167).

[26] Members have issued a document explicitly stating that they are in agreement with a few procedural initiatives regarding enhanced third party rights, and access to confidential information see WTO Docs. JOB/DSB/1 and JOB/DSB/1/Add. 4 of July 18, 2016.

[27] McDougall discusses the subject matter of the DSU Review in detail. Robert McDougall. 2018. The Crisis in WTO Dispute Settlement: Fixing Birth Defects to Restore Balance, Journal of World Trade, 52: 867–96.

[28] Compare the thoughts of Davey, that he has advanced in two separate publications which ask roughly the same question as we do here, but from different angles, William J. Davey. 2003. Has the WTO Dispute Settlement Exceeded its Authority? A Consideration of Deference Shown by the System to Member Government Decisions and its Use of Issue-Avoidance Techniques, pp. 43–80 in Thomas Cottier, Petros C. Mavroidis and Patrick Blatter (eds.). The Role of the Judge in International Trade Regulation, Experience and Lessons for the WTO, University of Michigan

What is the guarantee that this will be repeated in future practice? This brings us squarely into the discussion of precedent. We have already discussed the relevance of GATT panel reports, adopted as well as un-adopted. In what follows, we fold this discussion into the manner in which WTO courts have addressed precedent, both prior WTO as well as GATT courts' reports. It is of course in any court's interest to be consistent anyway, since its credibility is lost or at least eviscerated, if it serves one sauce for the goose and another for the gander. In presence of similar facts, and assuming no change in law, consistency is incentive-compatible for the judiciary. But consistency is not per se a value, as one can be consistently wrong. No court would want that. Holmes (1991) once quipped:

> It is revolting to have no better reason for a rule of law than that it was so laid down in the time of Henry IV. It is still more revolting if the grounds upon which it was laid down have vanished long since, and the rule simply persists from blind imitation of the past. But as precedents survive like the clavicle in the cat, long after the use they once served is at an end, and the reason for them has been forgotten, the result of following them must often be failure and confusion from the merely logical point of view.[29]

Holmes has a point, for sure. Just pause for a moment, and think what the welfare implications for our societies would have been if, with respect to the treatment of vertical restraints, the world competition authorities had stopped the clock in 1911, and the Dr Miles judgment,[30] and closed their eyes to all evolution in economic thinking regarding the differences between inter- and intra-brand competition, and the consequential need for affording these two forms of competition a different legal treatment.

Even though a concept associated with common law, precedent (*stare decisis*, that is, to stand by things decided) does not amount to an imperative to never change. It is, rather, a question of who has the right to deviate from past decisions, and under what conditions. The authority to deviate is entrusted to the highest court. The conditions vary, and the range encompasses new theories (as in Dr Miles), as well as distinguishing factors. Recently, in *Ramos*

Press: Ann Arbor, Michigan; and William J. Davey. 2015. The First Years of WTO Dispute Settlement: Dealing with Controversy and Building Confidence, pp. 353–62 in Gabrielle Marceau (ed.). A History of Law and Lawyers in the GATT/WTO, Cambridge University Press & the WTO: Geneva, Switzerland.

[29]   Oliver Wendell Holmes. 1991. The Common Law (revised edition), Dover Publications: Mineola, New York.

[30]   *Dr. Miles Medical Co. v. John D. Park & Sons Co.*, 220 U.S. 373 (1911), *Dr. Miles Medical Company v. John D. Park & Sons Company No. 72*; argued January 4, 5, 1911; decided April 3, 1911; 220 U.S. 373.

v. Louisiana,[31] the US Supreme Court, a staunch believer in precedential value of decisions, captured this point to perfection:

> Even if we accepted the premise that Apodaca established a precedent, no one on the Court today is prepared to say it was rightly decided, and stare decisis isn't supposed to be the art of methodically ignoring what everyone knows to be true. Of course, the precedents of this Court warrant our deep respect as embodying the considered views of those who have come before. But stare decisis has never been treated as "an inexorable command." And the doctrine is "at its weakest when we interpret the Constitution" because a mistaken judicial interpretation of that supreme law is often "practically impossible" to correct through other means. To balance these considerations, when it revisits a precedent this Court has traditionally considered "the quality of the decision's reasoning; its consistency with related decisions; legal developments since the decision; and reliance on the decision."

Paraphrasing Justice Marshall thus, the US Supreme Court will treat past case law "not as authority, but with respect".[32]

In civil law, there is no *stare decisis*, but there is a neighboring concept, "jurisprudence constante", which allows courts some flexibility as it does not dictate blind obedience to whatever has been decided before, without going to the other extreme either, that of total neglect of past jurisprudence.[33]

International law tribunals usually adjudicate disputes between common and civil law countries, and might have to walk on the tightrope between these two concepts (*stare decisis*; *jurisprudence constante*). The best of them will emulate what Rosenne (1965)[34] has captured to perfection, when stating (p. 56): "precedents may be followed or discarded, but not disregarded".

This comes very close to Justice Marshall's "authority" and "respect" metaphor. At the end of the day, precedents matter precisely because of the force of their reasoning, and not because of cult-like features. And reason evolves. In this vein, the US has expressed a vivid criticism against mechanical reproduction of prior rulings.[35] Thus few would disagree with the conclusion

---

[31]   590 US (2020), No. 18-5924.
[32]   *Thirty Hogsheds of Sugar v. Boyle*, 3 U.S. (9 Cranch) 191 at 198, 3 L. Ed. 701 at 703.
[33]   Algero (2005) provides an excellent discussion of the issue in Louisiana law, a state which is caught between the US common law tradition, and the European/French civil law legacy, see Mary Garvey Algero. 2005. The Sources of Law and the Value of Precedent: A Comparative and Empirical Study of a Civil Law State in a Common Law Nation, Louisiana Law Review, 65: 775–822.
[34]   Shabtai Rosenne. 1965. The Law and Practice of the International Court, Martinus Nijhoff Publishers: Dordrecht, The Netherlands.
[35]   The USTR (United States Trade Representative) issued a very detailed report criticizing the Appellate Body in this respect, see https://ustr.gov/about-us/policy-offices/press-office/press-releases/2020/february/ustr-issues-report-wto-appellate

that, assuming prior decisions are sound, and in the absence of distinguish-ing factors (not only factual differentiation, but also the emergence of new, improved theory), adherence to precedent is self-serving for the trading community, even if the WTO regime does not know of *stare decisis* (binding precedent). Has this been the case? We next turn to this issue, before asking in more aggregate terms what is the legal significance that WTO courts have attached to precedent.

1.6.1.   What is the emerging practice?

In Japan—Alcoholic Beverages II, the Appellate Body explicitly acknowl-edged that case law is transaction-specific, but, nevertheless, noted that an equivalent provision in the ICJ Statute did not prevent the ICJ from establish-ing its own jurisprudence (p. 13):

> It is worth noting that the Statute of the International Court of Justice has an explicit provision, Article 59, to the same effect. This has not inhibited the development by that Court (and its predecessor) of a body of case law in which considerable reliance on the value of previous decisions is readily discernible.

This report paved the way for what came next. In US—Shrimp (Article 21.5—Malaysia), the Appellate Body clarified the legal relevance of WTO panel and Appellate Body reports. In its view, the rationale for treating adopted GATT reports as part of the GATT acquis also applied to WTO reports (§102):

> This reasoning applies to adopted AB Reports as well. Thus, in taking into account the reasoning in an adopted AB Report—a Report, moreover, that was directly relevant to the Panel's disposition of the issues before it—the Panel did not err. The Panel was correct in using our findings as a tool for its own reasoning. Further, we see no indication that, in doing so, the Panel limited itself merely to examining the new measure from the perspective of the recommendations and rulings of the DSB.

Building on this case law, in US—Line Pipe, the Appellate Body explained that it would resort to its prior case law when, in the absence of other distinguishing features, the former and instant cases present factual similarities (§102). And in EC—Sardines, it included extensive references to prior case law in order to support its position that it has the legal authority to accept *amicus curiae* briefs (§§155–62). In US—Stainless Steel (Mexico), the Appellate Body, having first re-visited all prior case law, drew the operational consequences. In five

---

-body. A discussion of the US attitude is offered in Giorgio Sacerdoti. 2020. The Authority of "Precedent" in International Adjudication: The Contentious Case of the WTO's Appellate Practice, The Law and Practice of International Courts and Tribunals, 19: 497–514.

paragraphs (§§158–62), it underscored that it was expecting from subsequent panels to follow prior Appellate Body rulings, whenever appropriate. We quote the most telling passage in §161:

> The Panel's failure to follow previously adopted Appellate Body reports addressing the same issues undermines the development of a coherent and predictable body of jurisprudence clarifying Members' rights and obligations under the covered agreements as contemplated under the DSU. Clarification, as envisaged in Article 3.2 of the DSU, elucidates the scope and meaning of the provisions of the covered agreements in accordance with customary rules of interpretation of public international law. While the application of a provision may be regarded as confined to the context in which it takes place, the relevance of clarification contained in adopted Appellate Body reports is not limited to the application of a particular provision in a specific case.

In US—Continued Zeroing, it used even more explicit language (§362):

> Following the Appellate Body's conclusions in earlier disputes is not only appropriate, it is what would be expected from panels, especially where the issues are the same. This is also in line with a key objective of the dispute settlement system to provide security and predictability to the multilateral trading system. The Appellate Body has further explained that adopted panel and Appellate Body reports become part and parcel of the *acquis* of the WTO dispute settlement system and that "ensuring 'security and predictability' in the dispute settlement system, as contemplated in Article 3.2 of the DSU, implies that, absent cogent reasons, an adjudicatory body will resolve the same legal question in the same way in a subsequent case." Moreover, referring to the hierarchical structure contemplated in the DSU, the Appellate Body reasoned in *US—Stainless Steel (Mexico)* that the "creation of the Appellate Body by WTO Members to review legal interpretations developed by panels shows that Members recognized the importance of consistency and stability in the interpretation of their rights and obligations under the covered agreements." The Appellate Body found that failure by the panel in that case to follow previously adopted Appellate Body reports addressing the same issues undermined the development of a coherent and predictable body of jurisprudence clarifying Members' rights and obligations under the covered agreements as contemplated under the DSU.

Panels have by and large obliged. In US—Shrimp and Sawblades, the panel, noting first in §7.25 that it was dealing with yet another zeroing case, and in §7.28 that the Appellate Body had already condemned zeroing on numerous occasions, it went on to hold in §7.29 that, although the WTO legal order did not know of a formal *stare decisis*, the Appellate Body had cautioned against failure by panels to follow its reports addressing the same issue. In §7.30 then, the panel invoked the consistent line of reports condemning zeroing, and in §7.31 it held that, by invoking this case law, China had adduced *prima facie* evidence, which the US had not managed to rebut.[36] Panels will follow previous reports issued by the Appellate Body, either because they are genuinely persuaded by the reasoning, or because they mechanically adhere to prior case law in order to enhance legal security and predictability, and thus serve transaction-costs related arguments. The panel report on India—Patents (EC) eloquently captures this point (§7.30):

> Panels are not *bound* by previous decisions of panels or the Appellate Body even if the subject-matter is the same ... However, ... we will take into account the conclusions and reasoning in the Panel and Appellate Body reports in W T/DS50. Moreover, in our examination we believe that we should give significant weight to both Article 3.2 of the DSU, which stresses the role of the WTO dispute settlement system in providing security and predictability to the multilateral trading system, and to the need to avoid inconsistent rulings (which concern has been referred to by both parties). In our view, these considerations form the basis of the requirement of the referral to the "original panel" wherever possible under Article 10.4 of the DSU. (emphasis in the original)

Still, there are instances where panels did not follow prior rulings by the Appellate Body. In EC—Commercial Vessels, for example, the panel refused to adhere to the Appellate Body's understanding of Article 18.1 of the Agreement on Antidumping, which it had expressed in its report on US—Offset Act (Byrd Amendment). In similar vein, in Argentina—Preserved Peaches, the panel took distance from standing Appellate Body case law to the effect that safeguards can only be imposed if increased imports were the result of unforeseen developments[37] (§7.24):

> We do not agree with the statement by the Appellate Body in Argentina—Footwear (EC) that "the increased quantities of imports should have been 'unforeseen' or 'unexpected'." The text of Article XIX.1(a), together with the Appellate Body's own discussion of it and earlier conclusion regarding the logical connection between the circumstances in the first clause of Article XIX.1(a)—including unforeseen developments—and the conditions in the second clause—including an increase in imports—show that this is not a requirement for the imposition of a safeguard measure.

---

[36] Prusa and Vermulst provide an authoritative account of the case law on zeroing, see Thomas J. Prusa and Edwin Vermulst. 2009. A One-Two Punch on Zeroing: U.S.—Zeroing (EC) and U.S.—Zeroing (Japan), World Trade Review, 8: 187–241.

[37] A point that Sykes has persuasively criticized, see Alan O. Sykes. 2006. The WTO Agreement on Safeguards: A Commentary, Oxford University Press: New York City, New York.

Most of the activity regarding dissents from prior rulings is in the realm of zeroing.[38] A series of panels have distanced themselves from the Appellate Body's consistent outlawing of the zeroing practice in anti-dumping investigations. Still two subsequent panel reports, one by majority voting, namely US—Softwood Lumber V (Article 21.5—Canada), and one more recently unanimously so, US—Differential Pricing Methodology, have concluded the opposite.

By and large thus, panels have adhered to prior rulings by the Appellate Body. Has the Appellate Body followed its prior rulings? By and large again, this has been the case, even though there have been some notorious back and forth. The interpretation of "less favorable treatment" is a case to the point: from Korea—Various Measures on Beef, to Dominican Republic—Sale and Import of Cigarettes to EC—Seal Products, the relevance of the policy rationale to justify disparate trade effects has moved from relevance to irrelevance twice. In similar vein, the legal test to show that subsidies have passed through has changed a few times over, as we have shown in Grossman and Mavroidis (2007).[39] And there are a few other examples of the sort, but as already stated, similar examples constitute the exception rather than the rule. The problem is that WTO members are not making an overall evaluation of the record when deciding on the vote of confidence for WTO courts, but rather base their judgment primarily on their own experience. And if they have been on the receiving end of inconsistencies, then this is all that matters.

In C-267/91 and 268/91 (*Keck & Mithouard*), the Court of Justice of the EU was facing a question regarding restrictions on free movement of goods, an issue that it had decided dozens of times before. It had no problem accepting that its prior judgments had been in part at least, unwarranted and probably erroneous. In §16 of its judgment of November 24, 1993, the Court of Justice had no problem to explicitly admit that it had indeed erred when stating

> By contrast, contrary to what has previously been decided, the application to products from other Member States of national provisions restricting or prohibiting certain selling arrangements is not as to hinder directly or indirectly, actually or potentially, trade between Member states …

---

[38] We have included a comprehensive discussion of this case law in Chapter 11 of Petros C. Mavroidis. 2022. The WTO Dispute Settlement System, How, Why and Where? Edward Elgar Publishing: Northampton, Massachusetts and Cheltenham, United Kingdom.

[39] Gene M. Grossman and Petros C. Mavroidis. 2007. Recurring Misunderstanding of Non-Recurring Subsidies, US—Certain EC Products, pp. 381–90 in Henrik Horn and Petros C. Mavroidis (eds.). The WTO Case Law, The American Law Institute Reporters' Studies, Cambridge University Press: Cambridge, United Kingdom.

Compare this refreshing breath of intellectual honesty with the Appellate Body case law on less favorable treatment. In §146 of its report on Korea—Various Measures on Beef, disparate (trade) effects per se sufficed to find that Korea had afforded imported goods less favorable treatment than that reserved to their domestic counterparts. The Appellate Body saw no room for the relevance of the policy rationale for the Korean measure (arguably, the fight against illegal practices), and its potential justification of adverse effects. In Dominican Republic—Import and Sale of Cigarettes, the challenged measure was a "bond requirement". Cigarette importers had to post a bond to ensure payment of taxes. The level of the bond requirement depended on the market share in the Dominican market of the tobacco producer. It so happened that some foreign producers held a larger market share than their Dominican counterparts and were thus burdened with the payment of larger sums. Their complaint was that they were being afforded less favorable treatment. In §96 of its report, the Appellate Body held:

> The Appellate Body indicated in *Korea—Various Measures on Beef* that imported products are treated less favourably than like products if a measure modifies the conditions of competition in the relevant market *to the detriment of imported products*. However, the existence of a detrimental effect on a given imported product resulting from a measure does not necessarily imply that this measure accords less favourable treatment to imports if the detrimental effect is explained by factors or circumstances unrelated to the foreign origin of the product, such as the market share of the importer in this case. In this specific case, the mere demonstration that the per-unit cost of the bond requirement for imported cigarettes was higher than for some domestic cigarettes during a particular period is not, in our view, *sufficient* to establish "less favourable treatment" under Article III.4 of the of GATT 1994. (emphasis in the original)

Now, this looks like an about face, does it not? And yet, nothing like "we erred", or "contrary to what we have decided", prefaced this paragraph. And some might have legitimately thought that the above quoted passage had become the "new normal", as in its subsequent report on US—FSC (Article 21.5—EC), the Appellate Body held (§215):

> The examination of whether a measure involves "less favourable treatment" of imported products within the meaning of Article III.4 of the GATT 1994 must be grounded in close scrutiny of the "fundamental thrust and effect of the measure itself." This examination cannot rest on simple assertion, but must be founded on a careful analysis of the contested measure and of its implications in the marketplace. At the same time, however, the examination need not be based on the *actual effects* of the contested measure in the marketplace. (emphasis in the original)

But then came EC—Seal Products, and in §5.110, the Appellate Body travelled 180 degrees to return right back to where it had started from in Korea—Various Measures on Beef:

> In the light of the above, we do not agree with the European Union's reading of the Appellate Body's statement in EC—Asbestos. Specifically, we do not consider that the Appellate Body's statement that a Member may draw distinctions between imported and like domestic products without necessarily violating Article III.4 stands for the proposition that the detrimental impact of a measure on competitive opportunities for like imported products is not dispositive for the purposes of establishing a violation of Article III.4.

We will never know why the EU got it wrong when quoting from prior case law on "less favorable treatment", as the Appellate Body simply asserted that this had been the case with no further elaboration. What is clear, is that the presence of a detrimental impact in and of itself from that report onwards leads to a violation of Article III.4 of GATT. WTO members defending themselves against similar challenges will have to dig into the language of Article XX of GATT in order to justify their measures. The above is a far cry from the responsible treatment of precedent in the *Keck & Mithouard* judgment. Alas, it is not the only example.

1.6.2. Precedent is not a source of law, but …
To the extent that WTO courts have observed the agency contract included in Article 3.2 of the DSU, sticking to the precedent (as is the case in the vast majority of disputes) could lead to erroneous outcomes, but not to anything more. But to the extent that WTO courts have trespassed their mandate, then sticking to precedent is a perilous slippery slope, as repetitions of past jurisprudence would end up piling up the numbers of institutional deviations.

For the reasons explained above (the incompleteness of both the WTO contract, which is overwhelmingly full of standards as opposed to rules, as well as the incompleteness of the VCLT), recourse to VCLT is no safe way towards observing the agency contract, even if it is the contract itself that mandates its use.

5. Sources and general principles of (WTO) law: not sources, but ...

1. CUSTOM AND GENERAL PRINCIPLES OF LAW

Customs and general principles of law have served before international jurisdictions (and, especially, the ICJ) as autonomous sources of law. This is not the case for the WTO, as we explain in what now follows, even though, with respect to custom, there has been one occasion that briefly cast doubt on the accuracy of this statement. When it comes to the functionality of general principles, it is more appropriate to use them as a source of law, when the judge can adjudicate *ex aequo et bono*. This is the case for the ICJ judge, but not for the WTO adjudicator. And this is probably what explains why, in WTO practice, general principles have never been used as autonomous sources of (substantive) law, as we will see in what unfolds.

1.1. The Treatment of Customary International Law

As the above cited Article 38 of the Statute of the ICJ makes clear, customary international law is a source of law that the ICJ will routinely apply in disputes submitted to it. It consists of two elements, namely, state practice (referred to as *usus*), which must have been accepted as law (usually referred to as *opinio juris*).[1] The question we ask here is whether there is room for customary international law in the realm of WTO law. Is customary international law, in other words, de jure or de facto a source of WTO law?

The response to the first part of the question must be a resounding "no", as the DSU mentions only "covered agreements", and none of the legal institutions of the world trading edifice, not even MFN, as Jackson (1969) has concluded and state practice confirmed, is considered to be part and parcel of

---

[1] See the very comprehensive treatment of this issue, in Eyal Benvenisti. 2004. Customary International Law as Judicial Tool for Promoting Judicial Efficiency, pp. 85–116 in Eyal Benvenisti and Moshe Hirsch (eds.). The Impact of International Law on International Cooperation, Cambridge University Press: Cambridge, United Kingdom.

customary law. But what about the second question, namely whether de facto custom has emerged as a source of WTO law. How has practice addressed this issue?

WTO adjudicating bodies have not had many opportunities to speak on this issue. This observation, in and of itself, suggests that WTO members do not view custom as an independent source of rights and obligations in the realm of the WTO, neither de jure nor de facto. The panel on Korea—Procurement emerges as the only instance in WTO case law where a comprehensive discussion regarding the relevance of customary international law in the WTO legal order has ever taken place. This dispute concerned an alleged violation by Korea of its obligations under the WTO GPA (Government Procurement Agreement). In this context, the panel also had to deal with a non-violation complaint, a complaint, that is, that benefits accruing to a member have been nullified, even if the respondent had not violated its WTO obligations. The panel, for whatever reason, proceeded to examine this GATT/WTO legal institution (non-violation complaint) in the light of customary international law—and more specifically, in relation to *pacta sunt servanda* ("agreements must be kept").[2] One might legitimately ask whether it was at all necessary to proceed in this way. Still the panel did as much, and held that:

> Customary international law applies generally to the economic relations between the WTO Members. Such international law applies to the extent that the WTO treaty agreements do not "contract out" from it. To put it in another way, to the extent that there is no conflict or inconsistency, or an expression in a covered WTO agreement that implies differently, we are of the view that the customary rules of international law apply to the WTO treaties and to the process of treaty formation under the WTO.

In a few lines, the panel suggested that general customary international law is always relevant, unless the covered agreements have explicitly contracted out from it. The natural consequence would be that, since the content of customary international law contains elements additional to WTO contractual rights and obligations, customary international law must also be considered a source of WTO law. It is unclear whether the panel was referring to customary international law binding all of the membership, or whether it had opened the door to asymmetric obligations in this context. After all, regional customary international law does exist, and has been recognized as such by the ICJ.[3]

---

2   Through this instrument, a complainant challenges legal practices by the respondent, which still cause trade damage.
3   Alberto Alvarez-Jimenez. 2011. Identification of Customary International Law in the International Court of Justice's Jurisprudence, 2000–2009, The International and Comparative Law Quarterly, 60: 681–712.

Recall that Pauwelyn[4] has argued that WTO law is a part of a wider whole, the whole being public international law. He would certainly have approved of this panel report. And of course, if this approach entailed simply the use of interpretative elements from the wider public international law, then few would have argued with it. If, however, the suggestion is that by referring to customary international law, we are looking for autonomous sources of law additional to the covered (and the incorporated) agreements, then the discussion become tricky, at least.

Identification of the relevant customary international law is a concern in and of itself: which customary international law is relevant? To respond to this question, we need a precise definition of the customary international law (other than *jus cogens*, of course) that binds all 164 WTO Members. And what about those that will accede in the future? Of course, different WTO members observe different customs. One would have to accept that WTO members have accepted asymmetric obligations, were one to open the door to custom as autonomous source of law. Asymmetry is one concern. The other is proof of custom. No custom has been incorporated in WTO law, and judges would have to look elsewhere. But they cannot look "elsewhere" to identify WTO sources of law, as a result of Article 1 of the DSU that we have already discussed. So, what to do? Legal uncertainty will unavoidably increase if the WTO door was opened to accepting customary international law as an autonomous source of law.

Some of customary international law has been codified: the VCLT, the UN General Assembly resolution on state responsibility, and the 1982 Convention on the Law of the Sea are very appropriate illustrations. The latter could be relevant for the discussion of rules of origin, though at this stage there is nothing like a substantive agreement on rules of origin in the WTO. The General Assembly resolution on state responsibility has been referred to in some WTO disputes, and extensively in the Arbitrator's report on US—FSC (Article 22.6—US), where it was used as supplementary means to support the interpretative decision on remedies, and not as an autonomous source of law.[5] The panel on EC—Hormones held the view that, assuming *arguendo* that the precautionary principle is customary international law, it would not override explicit provisions of the covered agreements. This conclusion was affirmed by the Appellate Body (§§120–25).

---

[4]   Pauwelyn (2003) op. cit. Compare, Anna Ventouratou. 2021. The Law on State Responsibility and the World Trade Organization, The Journal of World Investment & Trade, 22: 759–803.

[5]   Ventouratou (2021) op. cit., discusses this issue in sufficient detail.

The Korea—Procurement went one step further pronouncing the (potential) relevance of all customary international law, absent explicit contracting out from it. Nevertheless, we suggest that it would be wrong to conclude that customary international law matters in WTO law, based on this observation. The report remains an outlier, and its suggested approach has not been endorsed by the Appellate Body either. The quoted passage concerns practically an issue of little if any relevance to the eventual outcome of the dispute. Indeed, irrespective whether non-violation complaints find support in customary international law, they are treaty language anyway, and have their place in the WTO legal order.

In subsequent cases, panels have rarely, if ever, referred to customary law, and when they did so, it was consistently in order to confirm a conclusion that they had already reached. Custom, we can conclude, is not only de jure but also de facto not a source of WTO law, as things stand.

1.2.   General Principles of Law[6]

General principles are an amorphous category comprising a range of legal norms: from good faith to *res judicata* and estoppel, various general principles have been routinely used in international adjudication, WTO courts included.

Article 38 of the Statute of ICJ mentions "general principles" among the sources of law that the ICJ can draw from. The ICJ has in practice used, on occasion, general principles of law as a source of law, when faced with gaps in contractual language or customary practice, and based their decisions on their understanding of their content. Higgins (1994) provides an excellent account to this effect.[7]

Unlike the ICJ though, WTO courts have never used a general principle as a source of law, as autonomous base, that is, to decide disputes before them. Recourse to general principles of law has been consistently used as means to

---

[6]   Here we draw on our prior attempts to address this issue, N. David Palmeter and Petros C. Mavroidis. 1998. The WTO Legal System: Sources of Law, American Journal of International Law, 92: 398–413. A more succinct account is offered in N. David Palmeter, Petros C. Mavroidis and Niall Meagher. 2022. Dispute Settlement in the World Trade Organization, Practice and Procedure, 3rd edition, Cambridge University Press: Cambridge, United Kingdom.

[7]   Rosalyn Higgins. 1994. Problems and Process: International Law and How We Use It, Clarendon Press: Oxford, United Kingdom. Originally though, general principles of law, were used as supplementary means of interpretation see on this score Hersch Lauterpacht. 1927. Private Law Sources and Analogies in International Law, Longmans, Green & Co.: New York City, New York. See also Bin Cheng. 1953. General Principles of Law Applied by International Courts and Tribunals, Stevens & Sons, Ltd.: London, United Kingdom.

confirm an interpretation that panels had already arrived at, as "supplementary means of interpretation", that is. Various principles have been discussed (and on occasion acknowledged as relevant) in WTO jurisprudence, the majority of which are of a procedural nature.

1.2.1. Estoppel (claim preclusion)

Estoppel (a common law concept) is roughly understood in international practice as the practice that prevents ("estops") a party from making an assertion and/or bringing a particular claim/complaint, if another party which is the recipient of a promise has in good faith relied on it.[8] If its constituent elements have been met, international courts will refrain from exercising jurisdiction.

Already in the GATT years, the panel on EEC (Member States)—Bananas I, had found that estoppel can (§361) "result from the express, or in exceptional cases implied consent of the complaining parties".

And this is the key difference of estoppel from *res judicata*, which presupposes a court decision. Estoppel can, in other words, be the consequence of *res judicata*, but can arise out of extra-judicial conduct as well.

The first comprehensive discussion of "estoppel" appeared already in the GATT panel report on US—Softwood Lumber II. The parties to the dispute (Canada and the United States) had concluded a memorandum of understanding (MOU), and the question before the panel, inter alia, concerned the extent to which the parties, by signing the MOU, had waived their rights under the GATT and were thus estopped from any further action. The panel saw the principle of estoppel as having relevance within the GATT legal framework, when it held in §312:

> The Panel considered that, for purposes of determining whether the MOU was covered by Article 4:5(a) of the Agreement, the key question was whether in concluding the MOU Canada and the United States had intended to act under this provision.

To the extent that the common intention of the parties was to act upon the MOU, the panel was prepared to acknowledge the relevance of estoppel. In the subsequent paragraphs, the panel refuted this argument. The legal test for estoppel though, had been established there and then.

In Guatemala—Cement II, Mexico introduced a new complaint against the same practice that it had challenged already in Guatemala—Cement I. Guatemala argued that Mexico was estopped from pursuing that new com-

---

[8] Estoppel in international law is notoriously imprecise, see Christopher Brown. 1996. A Comparative and Critical Assessment of Estoppel in International Law, University of Miami Law Review, 50: 369–412.

plaint. The panel disagreed, reasoning that the estoppel principle is relevant only if the complaining party had clearly consented to the particular behavior in question, which Mexico had not done (§§823–4 and footnote 791). While the first time Mexico did not prevail because of procedural errors that it had committed in formulating its claims, Mexico never conceded anything to Guatemala. It reformulated its complaint, hoping that the panel would move now and discuss the case on its merits, something it had not done the first time.

Along the same lines, the panel on Argentina—Poultry Anti-dumping Duties reviewed the estoppel principle as a source restraining its jurisdiction. Argentina had argued that Brazil was estopped from submitting their dispute to a WTO panel, since the very same dispute had already been adjudicated by a MERCOSUR panel (the regional integration scheme in which both Argentina and Brazil participate). The panel dismissed Argentina's argument because, inter alia, in its view, Article 3.2 of DSU did not require panels to rule in any particular way and thus to conform their own decisions to those by other adjudicating bodies. The panel, however, seems to have accepted the parameters of the estoppel principle as presented by Argentina, namely, that estoppel arises in circumstances where a party makes a statement that is clear and unambiguous, voluntary, unconditional, authorized, and relied on by the other party in good faith (§§7.37–8).

Even though not explicitly couched in terms of estoppel, the panel on India—Autos faced an argument by India, that a claim had been inappropriately brought before it, since the EU (complainant) and India (defendant) had already reached a mutually agreed solution (MAS).[9] India was supposed to have removed a series of measures which formed the basis of the complaint by the EU. India argued that it was supposed to eliminate the measures by April 2001, that is, more than six months after the establishment of the panel. The panel found that no MAS had ever been concluded with respect to some of the measures before it, but had it been the case, it would have refrained from exercising jurisdiction (§§7.116–24). Now, if it walks like a duck ... This ruling certainly looks like estoppel alright.

These types of cases, where a claim of estoppel followed a bilateral solution that had been reached, became the template. Another pertinent example is Brazil—Aircraft (Article 22.6—Brazil), where the panel noted that an agreement had been concluded between the two parties at a DSB meeting not to

---

[9]   Mutually agreed solutions (MAS) can be reached at any stage of the process: in Japan—Quotas on Laver for example, an MAS between Korea and Japan was reached only four days before the issuance of the interim report, that is, some weeks after the issuance of the descriptive part of the panel report. It was notified to the panel which concluded its work by reporting that a MAS had effectively been reached (see §§14ff. in WTO Doc. WT/DS323/R).

seek countermeasures pending the report by the compliance panel on whether implementation had occurred. In its view, this agreement was binding on the parties to the dispute, and it did not include any findings on this issue (§3.8).

In presence thus of a binding agreement to settle a dispute, WTO panels have refrained from exercising jurisdiction. It bears repeating that none of the aforementioned cases qualify as *res judicata*, as no WTO panel had previously adjudicated a dispute. These are cases where either a MOU or a MAS had been concluded. Refusing to entertain a complaint thus amounts to panels implementing the "estoppel" principle.

Lack of clarity regarding the content of a MAS or a MOU is fatal for the party claiming estoppel. In EC—Bananas III (Article 21.5—Ecuador II), the panel faced an argument by the EU that Ecuador was legally barred from bringing a compliance challenge against it, since they had concluded together the "Bananas Understanding". The panel decided that Ecuador was not barred from challenging the EU measures (§7.75):

(a)   the Bananas Understanding provided only for a means, i.e., a series of future steps, for resolving and settling the dispute;
(b)   the adoption of the Bananas Understanding was subsequent to recommendations, rulings and suggestions by the DSB; and
(c)   parties had made conflicting communications to the WTO concerning the Bananas Understanding.

The panel went on to state that, in light of its conclusions above, the "Bananas Understanding" would not bar Ecuador from challenging the EU measures, even if it qualified as a mutually agreed solution (§7.135). Lack of clarity as to what exactly the bilateral compromise had been persuaded the panel that there was no room for estoppel. It did not exclude though, that it would have concluded otherwise, had there been a clear implementation by the EU of the "Bananas Understanding".

Estoppel can also be the consequence of a unilateral act (promise). Unilateral declarations, if made in the right context, have been considered binding both in public international law, as well as in WTO law.[10] In US—Section 301 Trade Act, the panel held in §7.112:

> In the SAA the US Administration indicated its interpretation of Sections 301–310 as well as the manner in which it intends to use its discretion under Sections 301–310, as follows (emphases added):
> "Although it will enhance the effectiveness of section 301, the DSU does not require any significant change in section 301 *for investigations that involve an alleged*

---

[10]   An appropriate illustration of the former is offered by the Nuclear Tests case (*Australia v. France*) 1974 ICJ Rep. 253, and Nuclear Tests case (*New Zealand*

violation of a Uruguay Round agreement or the impairment of U.S. benefits under such an agreement. In such cases, the Trade Representative will:
- invoke DSU dispute settlement procedures, as required under current law;
- base any section 301 determination that there has been a violation or denial of U.S. rights under the relevant agreement on the panel or Appellate Body findings adopted by the DSB;
- following adoption of a favourable panel or Appellate Body report, allow the defending party a reasonable period of time to implement the report's recommendations; and
- if the matter cannot be resolved during that period, seek authority from the DSB to retaliate (emphasis added).

This official statement in the SAA—in particular, the commitment undertaken in the second bullet point—approved by the US Congress in the expectation that it will be followed by future US Administrations, is a major element in our conclusion that the discretion created by the statutory language permitting a determination of inconsistency prior to exhaustion of DSU proceeding has effectively been curtailed. As we already noted, we find that this decision of the US Administration on the manner in which it plans to exercise its discretion, namely to curtail it in such a way so as never to adopt a determination of inconsistency prior to the adoption of DSB findings, was lawfully made under the statutory language of Section 304.

Based thus on the US employing its domestic legislation in a manner consistent with the obligations it had assumed under the WTO, the panel rejected the EU complaint. Two caveats are in order. First, the Appellate Body did not speak on this issue, that is, on whether estoppel applies in cases where a unilateral declaration has been made that a certain conduct would be followed in future practice. The panel report was not appealed. Second, the unilateral declaration made by the US was grounds for the panel to reject a claim, and not to refrain from exercising jurisdiction. There is no case so far where a party has been denied jurisdiction because of a binding unilateral declaration. Still, the logic applied in the panel on US—Section 301 of the Trade Act, if confirmed, will be relevant in a case that could give rise to "estoppel": the EU would be legitimized to rely in good faith on similar declaration.

Against this background, the Appellate Body had for the first time the opportunity to present its views on estoppel, in general manner, in its report on EC—Export Subsidies on Sugar. Noting that it had never applied this principle in prior case law, it took the view that, if relevant at all, the principle had been narrowed down to Articles 3.7 and 3.10 DSU. These two provisions require WTO members to exercise their judgment as to the fruitfulness of submitting a dispute, and attempt reconciliation as well. And it was left at that. Unlike

---

v. France) 1974 ICJ Rep. 457, see the discussion in Alfred P. Rubin. 1977. The International Legal Effects of Unilateral Declarations, American Journal of International Law, 71: 1–30; the analogous case in the WTO is the panel report on US—Section 301 Trade Act.

prior panels thus which constructed estoppel (almost) in line with the under-standing of this principle in public international law, the Appellate Body saw only a very narrow place for it within the space occupied by Articles 3.7 and 3.10.

The Appellate Body first noted in §310: "We agree with the Panel that it is far from clear that the estoppel principle applies in the context of WTO dispute settlement".

It further noted the divergence of views across the disputing parties regard-ing the content of estoppel, implying that disagreements about its content were a possible explanation for the lack of incorporation of this principle in the WTO legal order. And then, in §312, it afforded its *coup de grâce* on the future relevance of the principle in the WTO legal order:

> The principle of estoppel has never been applied by the Appellate Body. Moreover, the notion of estoppel, as advanced by the European Communities, would appear to inhibit the ability of WTO Members to initiate a WTO dispute settlement proceed-ing. We see little in the DSU that explicitly limits the rights of WTO Members to bring an action: WTO Members must exercise their "judgement as to whether action under these procedures would be fruitful", by virtue of Article 3.7 of the DSU, and they must engage in dispute settlement procedures in good faith, by virtue of Article 3.10 of the DSU. This latter obligation covers, in our view, the entire spectrum of dispute settlement, from the point of initiation of a case through implementation. Thus, even assuming arguendo that the principle of estoppel could apply in the WTO, its application would fall within these narrow parameters set out in the DSU.

In the next paragraphs, the Appellate Body entertained the argument advanced by the EU that lack of reaction by complainants about its subsidies programs amounted to acquiescence. Since they had acquiesced, complainants were estopped from complaining about them. The Appellate Body outright refuted the relevance of this argument, which could not be squared with the wording of Articles 3.7 and 3.10.

The analysis of the Appellate Body is not very persuasive. The two provi-sions mentioned (Articles 3.7 and 3.10) are rather "esoteric", as they request that members exercise judgment before submitting a dispute. Estoppel is an obstacle to submitting a claim, and any form of judgment regarding the fruit-fulness of an eventual submission is simply irrelevant. This case law seems to have closed the door to welcoming "estoppel" in the WTO legal order. Furthermore, what about cases where an MAS/MOU has been concluded? These cases can hardly come under Articles 3.7 or 3.10 DSU. And what is the incentive to conclude a MAS/MOU, if litigation can start from scratch, its presence notwithstanding? The Appellate Body would have to re-think its attitude on this score, it seems to us at least.

1.2.2. *Res judicata* (matter decided)

Res judicata is widely practiced in both national as well as international adjudication. The panel on India—Autos discussed *res judicata* extensively, holding that the principle has its place in the WTO legal order. This panel made it clear that there are stringent conditions attached to this principle, namely (§§7.54–66):

(a)   the measures challenged in the original and the subsequent disputes must be identical;
(b)   the claims in the two disputes must be identical as well; and
(c)   the parties in the two disputes must be identical.

If these three conditions have been cumulatively met, then *res judicata* comes into play. This benchmark is largely consonant with the understanding of this principle in public international law.

1.2.3. Error

The panel on Korea—Procurement is the only report that contains a comprehensive discussion of error, as understood in customary international law, and codified in Article 48 of VCLT. Strictly speaking, there was no need for the panel to delve into this question, as the dispute between the US and Korea centered around the question whether an entity had been covered in Korea's offer when it had adhered to the WTO Government Procurement Agreement (GPA). The panel could have responded in the negative, and leave it at that. Instead, it added to its response a reference to customary international law, as codified in Article 48 of VCLT, which reads:

1.   A State may invoke an error in a treaty as invalidating its consent to be bound by the treaty if the error relates to a fact or situation which was assumed by that State to exist at the time when the treaty was concluded and formed an essential basis of its consent to be bound by the treaty.
2.   Paragraph 1 shall not apply if the State in question contributed by its own conduct to the error or if the circumstances were such as to put that State on notice of a possible error.
3.   An error relating only to the wording of the text of a treaty does not affect its validity; article 79 then applies.

In the case at hand, the panel, having found that the US had erroneously believed that the Korean entity was an integral part of the Korean offer, proceeded to decide whether Korea had contributed to the error (which, if correct, would have led to Korea's culpability). Citing substantial circumstantial evidence, it concluded that this had not been the case (§§7.120 et seq.). The panel's analysis is sound, but one might legitimately wonder whether it was equally functional (necessary).

More to the point, this remains the only case which discussed error as under-stood in customary international law. In similar cases, where panels and the Appellate Body were asked to pronounce on the actual content of a concession, they have either tried to establish the common intention of the negotiating parties (EC—Computer Equipment), or delved into the negotiating record to find out what exactly had been agreed (Canada—Dairy), and/or assumed the task of interpreting the tariff concession agreed (EC—Chicken Cuts), without also asking whether an error had been committed, and who was responsible for that.

1.2.4.   *Exceptio non adimplenti contractus* **(exception due to contractual breach)**

In Argentina—Poultry Anti-dumping Duties Argentina had argued, inter alia, that other WTO members had been practicing what Argentina was being accused of, but without being punished. Argentina was arguing, in effect, that it should not be punished since others were also not respecting the relevant part of the WTO contract. Argentina was seeking, for all practical purposes, an exit from its contractual obligations, since other WTO members had already exited as well.

The panel responded that the dispute before it concerned only Argentina's practices, and not that of others (§7.79):

> Argentina asserts that the methodology used by the [Department of Unfair Trading Practices and Safeguards] has also been used by other WTO Members. Even assum-ing for the sake of argument that Argentina is correct, this argument is nevertheless irrelevant. In this dispute, we must determine the conformity of Argentina's meth-odology (and not that of other WTO Members) in light of the relevant provisions of the *[Anti-dumping] Agreement*. (emphasis in the original)

There is of course, nothing wrong with this response. The more complete response would have been that there is no room for this principle in the context of a multilateral contract. Even self-help in the WTO (suspension of conces-sions) is not a bilateral device, but requires multilateral authorization under Article 22.6 of DSU.

1.2.5.   *Bona fides* **(good faith)**

Numerous reports refer to the obligation to perform the WTO treaty in good faith, another customary international law principle that has been codified in Article 26 of VCLT (*pacta sunt servanda*), which reads: "Every treaty in force is binding upon the parties to it and must be performed by them in good faith".

Usually, the reference to good faith (*bona fides*) is *pro forma*, with no further explanation. This principle is well-embedded in all legal orders, as the opposite (bad faith) is synonymous with undoing a functioning legal order.

There are numerous references to this principle in various reports, all of them referring to good faith as the paramount obligation to implement assumed obligations. It is thus maybe more warranted to refer to the case law delineating the ambit of the principle. Case law has made it clear that any violation of a provision necessarily amounts to bad faith behavior. In a controversial report dealing with payments to the domestic industry supporting anti-dumping petitions, the Appellate Body explained itself on this score (§298).

US—Offset Act (Byrd Amendment) concerned a challenge against a US measure that promised payments to those private agents who would support a petition to initiate an anti-dumping investigation, in an effort to meet the threshold criteria established in the Agreement on Anti-dumping. Article 5.4 of the agreement reads:

> The application shall be considered to have been made "by or on behalf of the domestic industry" if it is supported by those domestic producers whose collective output constitutes more than 50 per cent of the total production of the like product produced by that portion of the domestic industry expressing either support for or opposition to the application. However, no investigation shall be initiated when domestic producers expressly supporting the application account for less than 25 per cent of total production of the like product produced by the domestic industry.

The Appellate Body (§§281 et seq.) in a long-winded statement (of dubious intellectual coherence, we might add) understood the term "expressing ... support" as outcome- and not process-oriented. It is not, in other words, the manner that counts in which the statutory thresholds have been met, it is only the outcome that matters. The US could, in other words, influence the outcome (support for a petition) by offering a carrot to supporters (payments in case duties were imposed). It is at least debatable, if not improbable altogether, that the negotiators were thinking along the lines suggested by the US when negotiating this provision of the Agreement on Anti-dumping. The Appellate Body reduced the good faith obligation to a mere observance of the statutory threshold, allowing admittedly bad efforts to manipulate the process and arrive at the threshold itself.

This ruling remains, thankfully, an isolated incident. It is evidence though, of a point that Zoller (1977) first made, and Virally (1983) underscored: alas, even though this principle is ubiquitous in international judgments, only vague (and sometimes unsubstantiated, as in the case of the Appellate Body ruling discussed above) explanations of the principle have been offered.[11]

---

[11] Elizabeth Zoller. 1977. La Bonne Foi en Droit International, Pedone: Paris, France; Michel Virally. 1983. Review Essay: Good Faith in Public International Law, American Journal of International Law, 77: 130–34.

1.2.6. *In dubio mitius* (more leniently in case of doubt)

The *in dubio mitius* principle has been invoked in more than one case, the leading case being the EC—Hormones AB report (§§154–65). The dispute concerned the conformity of an EU legislation banning sales of hormone-treated beef in the EU market, for fear of comporting health externalities for consumers.

The Appellate Body reversed the panel's understanding concerning the allocation of the burden of proof when a WTO member deviates from an international standard mentioned in the Agreement on Sanitary and Phyto-Sanitary (SPS) Measures. Contrary to what the panel had held, the Appellate Body took the view that an adjudicating body cannot simply assume that, in presence of two possible readings of the same provision, WTO members opted for the relatively more onerous of the two.

To reach this conclusion, the Appellate Body developed its understanding of the maxim *in dubio mitius* (§165):

> We cannot lightly assume that sovereign states intended to impose upon themselves the more onerous, rather than the less burdensome, obligation by mandating *conformity* or *compliance with* such standards, guidelines and recommendations. To sustain such an assumption and to warrant such a far-reaching interpretation, treaty language far more specific and compelling than that found in Article 3 of the *SPS Agreement* would be necessary. (emphasis in the original)

Citing numerous public international law books and articles that discuss the principle *in dubio mitius*, the Appellate Body noted that this interpretative principle (which originates in criminal law) is widely recognized in international law as a "supplementary means of interpretation".

This concludes our discussion on the identification of, and the manner in which, general principles of international law have been understood in WTO practice. Recall, none of them has been explicitly mentioned in the covered agreements. It is the WTO courts that have introduced them in the legal vernacular of the world trading system. With the exception of the panel findings in Korea—Procurement (the approach of which has been discarded in subsequent practice), recourse to general principles of law has been consistently made under the guise of supplementary means of interpretation.

This brings us squarely into the discussion of the VCLT. The VCLT deals with the manner in which sources of law should be interpreted. When interpreting while following the VCLT rule, the interpreter has discretion to move beyond the covered agreements. While, as per Article 3.2 of DSU, it cannot add to the sources of law which must be strictly confined to the "covered agreements", the interpreter can use and has used extra WTO law to interpret the WTO sources of law. Which law it has used, is the subject of the next chapter.

6. The interpretative elements of WTO sources of law

1. INTERPRETING THE WTO SOURCES OF LAW THROUGH THE VCLT

Article 3.2 of the DSU identifies the interpretative method that adjudicating bodies must use: they must reach their interpretations using "customary" rules of interpretation. In its first ever report, in US—Gasoline, the Appellate Body equated the reference to customary rules embedded in Article 3.2 of DSU to the general rule of interpretation of VCLT (p. 17):

> That general rule of interpretation has attained the status of a rule of customary or general international law. As such, it forms part of the "customary rules of interpretation of public international law" which the Appellate Body has been directed, by Article 3(2) of the DSU, to apply in seeking to clarify the provisions of the General Agreement and the other "covered agreements" of the Marrakesh Agreement Establishing the World Trade Organization (the "WTO Agreement"). That direction reflects a measure of recognition that the General Agreement is not to be read in clinical isolation from public international law.

The VCLT is thus the means to honor the agency mandate included in Article 3.2 of DSU. The implicit belief of the framers, as argued already, must have been that, by obliging adjudicators to use customary rules of interpretation, they would be ensuring that agents would not be acting as principals, as they would not be undoing the balance of rights and obligations that the framers themselves had put together. WTO adjudicators, by equating the reference to customary rules to recourse to the VCLT, must have thought likewise. Their decision to do so has been met with wholehearted acquiescence by the membership of the WTO. No one has ever complained that the introduction of VCLT in adjudicatory practice has been inapposite.[1]

---

[1] Wetzel and Rauschning (1978), in their magnificent compilation of the *travaux préparatoires* (preparatory work) of VCLT, show that the framers of VCLT distilled carefully customary international law when drafting the VCLT, see Ralph Günther Wetzel and Dietrich Rauschning. 1978. The Vienna Convention on the Law of Treaties: Travaux Preparatoires, Metzner Verlag: Frankfurt am Main, Germany. Van Damme

The VCLT contains three provisions that govern interpretation of treaties:

- Article 31, entitled "General Rule of Interpretation";
- Article 32, "Supplementary Means of Interpretation";
- Article 33, "Interpretation of Treaties Authenticated in Two or More Languages".

Recourse to the VCLT accomplishes two important functions, since it affects both the extensive as well as the intensive margin of the interpretative elements used:

(a)   It is the road map to identifying the various interpretative elements, as terms like "context", "relevant rule of international law", "supplementary means of interpretation" are open-ended. It is through practice that these (and other terms appearing in the body of VCLT) will be dis-aggregated and specified. The extent of the extensive margin so to speak of the various interpretative elements, is in the hands of the WTO adjudicators;

(b)   By classifying an interpretative element under Article 31 or 32 of VCLT, the WTO adjudicator prejudges its legal intensity, the "intensive margin" of the interpretative elements, so to speak. If a bilateral agreement between the disputing parties, for example, is considered to be context of the covered agreements, then the judge has no choice, as it must take it into account. If, conversely, it is perceived to be supplementary means of interpretation, then recourse to it is a matter of discretion that the WTO adjudicator is free to exercise one way or the other (assuming a reading of Article 32 of VCLT, which denotes a hierarchy between the two provisions. We will return to this issue later).

1.1.   A Brief Primer on the VCLT

Article 31 of VCLT enumerates a list of elements that the judge/adjudicator must take into account when asked to interpret a legal canon:

- The text of the provision;
- its context;
- the object and purpose of the agreement;
- subsequent practice and agreement between the parties; as well as

---

(2009) provides a very comprehensive account of the manner in which WTO courts have had recourse to the VCLT, see Isabelle Van Damme. 2009. Treaty Interpretation by the WTO Appellate Body, Oxford University Press: Oxford, United Kingdom.

- any other relevant rules of international law.

Article 32 of the VCLT allows for recourse to supplementary means of interpretation in order to confirm the meaning that an adjudicator has reached through recourse to the elements included in Article 31, or in case prior recourse to these elements has left the meaning still obscure or ambiguous. Finally, Article 33 of VCLT addresses a special concern, namely, the question of treaty interpretation, when a treaty has been authenticated in two or more languages.

The VCLT is undeniably a useful tool, otherwise it would not have survived through hundreds of disputes in dozens of different contexts. It provides a balance across various elements that can help illuminate the meaning of terms agreed. As we will see in more detail in what follows, according to the VCLT, the terms of a treaty must be read in their context (the rest of the agreement, as well as other agreements signed and/or accepted by all signatories which are in connection with the agreement) taking into account the object and purpose of the agreement. Recourse to context is not only justified, but necessary indeed, as terms are not a-contextual. Words (terms) and paragraphs have meaning depending on the "rule of the game", a Wittgensteinian concept which comes close to the what the VCLT regime calls "context" in Article 31.[2] By respecting context no term will be over- or under-interpreted, and thus the principle of effective interpretation, the cornerstone of the VCLT, will be observed. By respecting context and object and purpose of the treaty, the interpreter will avoid teleological interpretations. Teleological interpretations have been consistently criticized for focusing on the ends sought (the object and purpose of treaty) and for disregarding the means committed to achieve the ends (the text and context), paying thus only lip service to the amount of national sovereignty transferred to the international plane. Context and object and purpose of the treaty help the interpreter interrogate why an agreement was signed, and what pathway has been chosen to achieve the objectives sought.

Recourse to subsequent practice/agreement of members will help judges/ adjudicators build a bridge between the historical past and modernity. State behavior (expressed through practice and/or new agreements) evolves, and it makes no sense at all to disregard and request signatories to return to a past they have abandoned. Relevant rules of international law can help in this way. And of course, even though moving to discuss the negotiating record is not compulsory, this does not mean that it is unnecessary. A lot, sometimes, can be learned, and a lot, by the same token, can be disregarded when judges pay no

---

[2]   Ludwig von Wittgenstein. 1953. Philosophical Investigations, Blackwell Publishing: Oxford, United Kingdom.

heed to it. Judges (and WTO adjudicators alike) are required to adjudicate one case at a time,[3] but they need to build a theory about the case, and the VCLT is a tool to help them build their scaffolding to this effect. Just think about it. Is the VCLT missing something?

Against this background, two separate issues arise when glancing through the VCLT:

- How should we understand the various terms appearing in the VCLT provisions?
- Is there a hierarchy between the elements included in Article 31 of VCLT, as well as between the two provisions (Articles 31, 32 of VCLT)?

We will take them in turn in what now follows.

1.1.1. Understanding the terms included in Articles 31 and 32 VCLT

Every term appearing in the body of Article 31 of the VCLT is prone to interpretation, even when a definition of the term has been provided.[4]

"Context" is interpreted in Article 31.2 of the VCLT as follows:

> The context for the purpose of the interpretation of a treaty shall comprise, in addition to the text, including its preamble and annexes:
> (a) any agreement relating to the treaty which was made between all the parties in connection with the conclusion of the treaty;
> (b) any instrument which was made by one or more parties in connection with the conclusion of the treaty and accepted by the other parties as an instrument related to the treaty.

Which agreements "relate" (a term which resembles an accordion) to the treaty at hand, is a judgment call, as are the instruments "in connection" with it.

And then there are terms mentioned in the body of the VCLT, which are not interpreted any further in the body of the VCLT. One might legitimately inquire into what is a relevant rule of international law? Disagreements can reasonably arise across well-intentioned individuals, when it comes to distinguishing wheat (relevant) from chaff (irrelevant rules of international law). Or,

---

[3] Sunstein has advanced very persuasive arguments in favor of minimalist judgments, see Cass R. Sunstein. 2001. One Case at a Time, Harvard University Press: Cambridge, Massachusetts.

[4] Villiger (2008) provides a comprehensive discussion of the VCLT, see Mark E. Villiger. 2008. Commentary on the 1969 Vienna Convention on the Law of Treaties, Brill Publishing: Leiden, the Netherlands.

different adjudicators could debate the content of subsequent practice/agreement, even though the Commentary to the VCLT does provide some guidance:

> The text provisionally adopted in 1964 spoke of practice which "establishes the understanding of all the parties." By omitting the word "all" the Commission did not intend to change the rule. It considered that the phrase "the understanding of the parties" necessarily means "the parties as a whole." It omitted the word "all" merely to avoid any possible misconception that every party must individually have engaged in the practice where it suffices that it should have accepted the practice.[5]

But the test does not respond to various questions which might arise in practice, such as, are informal agreements also included under "subsequent agreement"? How widespread, long, and consistent must practice be, to be considered subsequent practice?

All this is to say that the VCLT includes incomplete or no definitions of the terms it uses, which could give rise to legitimate divergence of view. The VCLT itself, to borrow from Justice Scalia, is "a matter of interpretation".[6]

1.1.2. Is there a hierarchy between the elements included in Article 31 of VCLT?

Jurists also differ to some extent in their basic approach to the interpretation of treaties according to the relative weight which they give to:

(a) The text of the treaty as the authentic expression of the intentions of the parties;

(b) The intentions of the parties as a subjective element distinct from the text; and

(c) The declared or apparent objects and purposes of the treaty.

Some place the main emphasis on the intentions of the parties and in consequence admit a liberal recourse to the *travaux préparatoires* and to the other evidence of the intentions of the contracting States as means of interpretation. Some give great weight to the object and purpose of the treaty and are in consequence more ready, especially in the case of general multilateral treaties, to admit teleological interpretations of the text which go beyond, or even diverge from, the original intentions of the parties as expressed in the text. The majority, however, emphasizes the primacy of the text as the basis for the interpretation of a treaty, while at the same time giving a certain place to extrinsic evidence of the intentions of the parties and to the objects and purposes of the treaty as means of interpretation.[7]

The above quoted passage is an excerpt from the Commentary to the VCLT. It is so true. Reputed international lawyers have gone so far as to suggest a

---

[5]   Wetzel and Rauschning (1978) op. cit., at p. 254.

[6]   Antonin Scalia. 1997. A Matter of Interpretation, Federal Courts and the Law, Princeton University Press: Princeton, New Jersey.

[7]   Wetzel and Rauschning (1978) op. cit., at p. 250.

"staggered" approach, where recourse to the elements of the VCLT should be warranted only if the text itself was not clear.[8] Of course, the clarity of the text is itself a matter of … interpretation. Lord Denning (2005), an eminent British jurist, warns against the tendency to look for the grammatical meaning, and asks from judges/adjudicators to inquire into "the evil which it was sought to remedy" (p. 10). As he explains (p. 9): "In doing this, you must of course start with the words used in the statute: but not end with them – as some people seem to think. You must discover the meaning of the words".[9]

Lord Denning did not have the WTO adjudicators in mind when writing these lines, even though his words seem particularly fitting since, as we will see, the WTO adjudicating bodies (and especially, the Appellate Body) have privileged textualism quite consistently. Wittgenstein might have undeniably been irritated with similar attitude.

Consequently, some do and some do not see a hierarchy, and the question legitimately arises whether there is one between the elements included in Article 31 of VCLT? The correct answer is that there is none. Quoting from the Commentary again:

> The Commission, by heading the article "General rule of interpretation" in the singular and by underlining the connexion between paragraphs 1 and 2 and again between paragraph 3 and the two previous paragraphs, intended to indicate that the application of the means of interpretation in the article would be a single combined operation. … it was consideration of logic, not any obligatory legal hierarchy, which guided the Commission …[10]

This is settled. But what is the coefficient of importance for each of the elements mentioned above? Depending on whether the judge pays more attention to text or context or the overarching purpose of the agreement for example, the outcome will vary.

---

[8]   Georges Abi-Saab, who served at the Appellate Body, understood the VCLT as a sequence of autonomous or discrete steps, see Georges Abi-Saab. 2010. The Appellate Body and Treaty Interpretation, pp. 99–109 in Malgosia Fitzmaurice, Olufemi Elias and Panos Merkouris (eds.). Treaty Interpretation and the Vienna Convention on the Law of Treaties: 30 Years On, Brill Publishers: Leiden, the Netherlands.

[9]   Alfred Thompson Denning. 2005.The Discipline of Law, Oxford University Press: Oxford, United Kingdom.

[10]   Wetzel and Rauschning (1978) op. cit., at pp. 251–2.

1.1.3. Is there a hierarchy between Articles 31 and 32 VCLT?

Article 32 of the VCLT, which is also part and parcel of customary international law, reads:

> Recourse *may* be had to supplementary means of interpretation, including the preparatory work of the treaty and the circumstances of its conclusion, in order to confirm the meaning resulting from the application of article 31, or to determine the meaning when the interpretation according to article 31:
> (a) leaves the meaning ambiguous or obscure; or
> (b) leads to a result which is manifestly absurd or unreasonable. (emphasis added)

Under a textual reading of this provision, the WTO judge does not have to delve into supplementary means. It has discretion to do so in order to confirm an interpretation reached, as he/she has discretion to decide whether one of the two conditions mentioned under (a) and/or (b) above, has been met. But sometimes the truth lies hidden in voluminous negotiating records, which might have to be thoroughly researched. Does the judge have unfettered discretion to use supplementary means of interpretation? Or is the drafting of Article 32 of the VCLT meant to denote something else?

Mortenson (2013), provides a brilliant account of the negotiating history of the VCLT to support the view that the final compromise should not be understood as some sort of demotion as far as the relevance of travaux to the interpretative exercise, is concerned. It was a carefully drafted compromise to ensure that the Myres McDougal viewpoint (that the text was of secondary importance), would be defeated. Consideration of *travaux préparatoires*, in Mortenson's careful account was never meant to become redundant.[11] His view seems to be the correct one, when reading the Commentary to the VCLT:

> … it is beyond question that the records of treaty negotiations are in many cases incomplete or misleading, so that considerable discretion has to be exercised in determining their value as an element of interpretation. Accordingly, the Commission was of the opinion that the distinction made in Articles 27 and 28 between authentic and supplementary means of interpretation is both justified and desirable. At the same time it pointed out that the provisions of Article 28 by no means have the effect of drawing a rigid line between the "supplementary" means of interpretation and the means included in Article 27. The fact that Article 28 admits recourse to the supplementary means for the purpose of "confirming" the meaning resulting from the application of Article 27 establishes a general link between the two articles and maintains the unity of the process of interpretation.[12]

---

[11] Julian Davis Mortenson. 2013. The Travaux of Travaux: Is the Vienna Convention Hostile to Drafting History? American Journal of International Law, 107: 780–822.
[12] Wetzel and Rauschning (1978) op. cit., at p. 252. Articles 27 and 28 in previous drafts, became Articles 31 and 32 respectively in the final version of the VCLT.

There it is then. There is a unity between the two provisions, and it is plain wrong to relegate recourse to Article 32 of the VCLT to mere option. In practice, recourse to *travaux préparatoires* in order to confirm a meaning is common currency across international tribunals,[13] and the WTO adjudicating bodies as well, as we will soon discover.

1.1.4.   Treaties authenticated in two or more languages
Finally, Article 33 VCLT is also of relevance (and the Appellate Body has made reference not only to Articles 31 and 32 of the VCLT), which deals with treaties signed in more than one language, and reads:

1. When a treaty has been authenticated in two or more languages, the text is equally authoritative in each language, unless the treaty provides or the parties agree that, in case of divergence, a particular text shall prevail.
2. A version of the treaty in a language other than one of those in which the text was authenticated shall be considered an authentic text only if the treaty so provides or the parties so agree.
3. The terms of the treaty are presumed to have the same meaning in each authentic text.
4. Except where a particular text prevails in accordance with paragraph 1, when a comparison of the authentic texts discloses a difference of meaning which the application of articles 31 and 32 does not remove, the meaning which best reconciles the texts, having regard to the object and purpose of the treaty, shall be adopted.

Article XVI of the Agreement Establishing the WTO acknowledges English, French, and Spanish to be authentic languages. But then, which version should be privileged in case of differences in the three texts? WTO adjudicating bodies, in the overwhelming majority of the cases, have used English as the working language.[14]

The Appellate Body has on occasion examined the French and the Spanish text to confirm a decision it had already reached while using the English text.[15] It has also clarified in US—Softwood Lumber IV that, in accordance with Article 33 of the VCLT, it should (§59): "seek the meaning that gives effect, simultaneously, to all the terms of the treaty, as they are used in each authentic language".

This approach would suggest that the treaty interpreter should privilege interpretations that overlap in the three different texts. But then, in its report on EC—Tariff Preferences (§147), the Appellate Body privileged the terms

---

[13]   Wetzel and Rauschning (1978) op. cit., at p. 255.
[14]   There are a few only exceptions, like the report on EC—Asbestos.
[15]   EC—Bed Linen, Appellate Body report at §123.

used in the French and the Spanish texts (which would roughly translate to "as defined"), which, to its own admission, reflected stronger, more obligatory language than the terms used in the English text (which would translate to "as described"). Recall that, under Article 33.4 of the VCLT, the interpreter has some latitude to choose the interpretation that best reconciles with the intended meaning of the text, as Article 33.3 only establishes a presumption to the effect that the terms have the same meaning across texts.

1.1.5. Does the VCLT always lead to one interpretation?

WTO adjudicating bodies, as we will see, behave in the overwhelming majority of times as if the response to this question must be in the affirmative.[16] And yet, those that put together the VCLT did not think so, or, at the very least, adopted a more nuanced approach:

> When a treaty is open to two interpretations one of which does and the other does not enable the treaty to have appropriate effects, good faith and the objects and purposes of the treaty demand that the former interpretation should be adopted.[17]

That much is clear, but what about instances where more than one interpretation enables a treaty to have appropriate effects? The VCLT does not respond to this question, and it does not exclude the possibility either. There are some extra-VCLT interpretative principles like *in dubio mitius* (leniency in case of doubt), that could offer help, but leniency toward whom? Take zeroing for example. Assume zeroing allows the Agreement on Anti-dumping to have appropriate effects. Should leniency work in favor of the party imposing duties, or the party suffering damage because of the duty imposition?

The discussion so far supports the view that, while the VCLT is a well-thought treaty which can help adjudicators to reach informed judgments, it is not panacea. In the hands of different judges, it might lead to hard-to-reconcile interpretations. The VCLT itself is an incomplete contract. Add to that that the WTO contract is full of standards and not rules, since it regulates the conduct of trading nations, and is a negative integration contract as well condoning regulatory diversity with respect to behind-the-border policies (instruments), and we can end up concluding that WTO adjudicators have quite a difficult task in their hands: they will be effectively asked to interpret one incomplete contract (WTO) through another incomplete contract (VCLT).[18] This is no small feat.

---

[16] They have, for example, only scarcely used the *in dubio mitius* (leniency in case of doubt) principle.

[17] Wetzel and Rauschning (1978) op. cit., at p. 251.

[18] Standards invite more judicial discretion than rules, the content of which is precise. On the distinction between "rules", and "standards", see Louis Kaplow. 1992. Rules Versus Standards: An Economic Analysis, Duke Law Journal, 42: 557–629.

In what follows, we will be referring to WTO practice, and how it has classified various interpretative elements under the headings of the VCLT (e.g., context, subsequent practice, etc.). Two conclusions emerge from the practice of WTO courts so far:

(a)   WTO adjudicating bodies have relied heavily on what they understand to be the ordinary meaning of the terms, and much less on elements such as context, state practice, or subsequent agreements;

(b)   When in doubt, they prefer to classify interpretative elements under supplementary means. This approach is obviously in line with their incentive structure to maintain maximum flexibility in the future; it is, unfortunately, on occasion, incorrect.

With this in mind, in this chapter we turn to practice. We want to first set the record straight, by inquiring into how WTO adjudicating bodies have understood the ambit of the constituent elements of the VCLT, and what kind of interpretative elements they have classified under each and every one of the various VCLT headings. Armed with this knowledge, we will turn in the next two chapters to the question whether by doing what they have done, WTO adjudicating bodies have observed the constitutional constraint, namely, to act as agents, and not as law-makers. It is there that we will try to illuminate the overall attitude of WTO adjudicators, and provide some suggestions regarding possible improvements.

1.2.   What is What in WTO Case Law?

In what follows, we discuss the manner in which WTO courts have classified the various interpretative elements that they have used in practice in order to interpret the covered agreements. We will place under the various VCLT headings (e.g., context, subsequent agreement/practice, etc.) the various elements (e.g., treaties, acts of international organizations) that WTO courts have used to interpret the covered agreements. There is, of course, no point in reproducing the instances where they have had recourse to the text of the agreement: what qualifies as "text" is self-interpreting, and recourse to it happens routinely in each and every report. Every time WTO courts refer, say, to Article I of GATT, they have interpreted this provision. In what now follows, we provide a list of the elements that WTO panels and the Appellate Body have used by classifying them under one of the remaining headings appearing in Articles 31 and 32 of the VCLT.

1.2.1. Context

The panel on EC—Chicken Cuts addressed a dispute between the EU and Brazil concerning the proper tariff classification of salted meat under the Harmonized System (HS) treaty of the World Customs Organization, the WCO (§119). To resolve their dispute, the panel had to first pronounce on the legal relevance of the HS treaty, an agreement which is not a covered agreement as the DSU understands this term.

The HS treaty, which provides a classification for all goods traded internationally, binds several WTO members that have formally ratified it, and is de facto observed by all WTO members. Unsurprisingly, various disputes involving claims regarding tariff-classification issues have mentioned the HS treaty. Until EC—Chicken Cuts, WTO courts, with the exception of innocuous statements (like that by the Appellate Body in §89 of its report on EC—Computer Equipment, to the effect that interpretation of schedules should be in line with the HS treaty), had not pronounced on the legal significance of HS treaty in the WTO legal order.

The Appellate Body, in its report on EC—Chicken Cuts, held that the HS treaty is context for the GATT in the sense of Article 31.2 of VCLT. The relevant passage reads (§199):

> The above circumstances confirm that, prior to, during, as well as after the Uruguay Round negotiations, there was broad consensus among the GATT Contracting Parties to use the Harmonized System as the basis for their WTO Schedules, notably with respect to agricultural products. In our view, this consensus constitutes an "agreement" between WTO Members "relating to" the WTO Agreement that was "made in connection with the conclusion of" that Agreement, within the meaning of Article 31(2)(a) of the Vienna Convention. As such, this agreement is "context" under Article 31(2)(a) for the purpose of interpreting the WTO agreements, of which the EC Schedule is an integral article. In this light, we consider that the Harmonized System is relevant for purposes of interpreting tariff commitments in the WTO Members' Schedules.

This classification of the HS treaty under "context" (in the sense of the VCLT) entails an immediate consequence: any time in subsequent practice the question of proper tariff classification arises, WTO courts will have to consult the HS (and its various interpretative rules).

The panel on Mexico—Telecoms relied heavily on a series of regulations and recommendations by the International Telecommunications Union (ITU) to clarify its understanding of "accounting rates" (§§7.129–136). At the heart of the dispute between Mexico and the United States was the question of the consistency of interconnection rates that the Mexican supplier, Telmex, was charging, with the WTO rules. The ITU regulation of accounting rates could provide important information in this respect. In support of its decision to move and discuss the content of various ITU instruments, the panel noted that:

- The ITU regulations were instruments binding both Mexico and the United States;
- the ITU recommendations were relevant since the parties to the dispute, as well as many other WTO members, were members of the ITU.

The ITU regulations had seen the light of day in 1988, a few years before the Telecoms Reference Paper (TRP), which addressed interconnection rates, had been adopted. Without explicitly saying so, this panel seems to have been treating the ITU regulations and recommendations as "historical" context of the TRP. It is also possible that it was treating it as supplementary means of interpretation, even though the discussion in the relevant paragraphs (§§7.129–136) does not support this conclusion.

There is of course, a marked difference between these two reports. It is the Appellate Body that explicitly conferred the status of "context" to the HS treaty. It is only a panel that implies that the ITU regulations enjoy the same status. There should be no question about the legitimacy of the Appellate Body finding, whereas it is probably wiser to await confirmation regarding the status of the ITU instruments in future practice.

1.2.2.   Subsequent agreement

Subsequent agreements are neither interpretations as per Article IX, nor amendments as per Article X of the Agreement establishing the WTO. They have distinct coverage, as they could concern a subject matter that had not been handled in the original contract. The subject matter of both interpretations as well as amendments is linked to an existing provision. That of a subsequent agreement can, but does not have to be linked to an existing provision.

In US—Clove Cigarettes, the Appellate Body (§§267–8) considered that §5.2 of the Doha Ministerial Decision was subsequent agreement in the sense of Article 31.3(a) of the VCLT. §5.2 reads as follows:

> subject to the conditions specified in paragraph 12 of Article 2 of the Agreement on Technical Barriers to Trade, the phrase "reasonable interval" shall be understood to mean normally a period of not less than 6 months, except when this would be ineffective in fulfilling the legitimate objectives pursued.

In §267, the Appellate Body revealed the quintessential reason why it had reached its conclusion the way it did:

> In this connection, we note that the understanding among Members with regard to the meaning of the term "reasonable interval" in Article 2.12 of the TBT Agreement

is expressed by terms—"shall be understood to mean"—that cannot be considered as merely hortatory.

The legal consequence of the characterization of §5.2 as subsequent agreement was presented in §269 of the Appellate Body report:

> We observe that, in its commentaries on the Draft articles on the Law of Treaties, the ILC states that a subsequent agreement between the parties within the meaning of Article 31(3)(a) "must be read into the treaty for purposes of its interpretation". As we see it, while the terms of paragraph 5.2 must be "read into" Article 2.12 for the purpose of interpreting that provision, this does not mean that the terms of paragraph 5.2 replace or override the terms contained in Article 2.12. Rather, the terms of paragraph 5.2 of the Doha Ministerial Decision constitute an interpretative clarification to be taken into account in the interpretation of Article 2.12 of the TBT Agreement.

In this case, thus, the subsequent agreement concerned an interpretation of an existing term. The reason why it was classified as "subsequent agreement" must be due to the fact that the process embedded in Article IX.2 of the Agreement Establishing the WTO had not been followed. From that dispute onwards, the (no less than) six-month period is how the term "reasonable interval" appearing in Article 2.12 of TBT should be understood.

Recently, the question has been raised whether subsequent agreements can be *inter se*, that is between a sub-set of the WTO membership, without reverting the form of a plurilateral agreement. Various members have gone ahead to negotiate JSIs (joint statement initiatives), where they either move into areas not covered by existing agreements (the part of the JSI on Investment Facilitation that concerns goods), or they enrich the multilateral legal framework with respect to existing agreements (the part of the JSI on Investment Facilitation that concerns services). The gambit of the participating WTO members has been criticized (if not excoriated) by those refusing to participate. WTO adjudicating bodies did not have to pronounce on this score at the moment of writing.[19]

1.2.3. Subsequent practice

Article 31 of VCLT refers to "any subsequent practice", without any further qualification. WTO case law seems to have adopted the view that only unanimous practice by all WTO Members could qualify as "subsequent practice". In its report on Japan—Alcoholic Beverages II, the Appellate Body held that

---

[19] A very recent contribution is dedicated precisely to this question, see Americo Beviglia-Zampetti, Patrick Low and Petros C. Mavroidis. 2022. Consensus Decision-Making and Legislative Inertia in the WTO: Can International Law Help? Journal of World Trade, 56: 1–26.

subsequent practice within the meaning of Article 31.3(b) of VCLT, exists when there is (p. 12): "'concordant, common and consistent' sequence of acts or pronouncements which is sufficient to establish a discernable pattern implying the agreement of the parties [to a treaty] regarding its interpretation".

In similar vein, in US—Gambling, the Appellate Body clarified that two elements must be simultaneously present, in order to be in presence of subsequent practice within the meaning of Article 31(3)(b) of VCLT (§192):

(a)   there must be a common, consistent, discernible pattern of acts or pronouncements; and
(b)   those acts or pronouncements must imply agreement on the interpretation of the relevant provision.

In EC—Computer Equipment, the Appellate Body included a critique of the panel's findings regarding the classification of LAN equipment, holding that it had not controlled for some important elements in reaching its decision. Importantly, the Appellate Body opened the door to acknowledging that decisions by the WCO HS Committee are being recognized as subsequent practice in the WTO legal order (§90):

> A proper interpretation also would have included an examination of the existence and relevance of subsequent practice. We note that the United States referred, before the Panel, to the decisions taken by the Harmonized System Committee of the WCO in April 1997 on the classification of certain LAN equipment as ADP machines. Singapore, a third party in the panel proceedings, also referred to these decisions. The European Communities observed that it had introduced reservations with regard to these decisions and that, even if they were to become final as they stood, they would not affect the outcome of the present dispute for two reasons: first, because these decisions could not confirm that LAN equipment was classified as ADP machines in 1993 and 1994; and, second, because this dispute "was about duty treatment and not about product classification". We note that the United States agrees with the European Communities that this dispute is not a dispute on the correct classification of LAN equipment, but a dispute on whether the tariff treatment accorded to LAN equipment was less favourable than that provided for in Schedule LXXX. However, we consider that in interpreting the tariff concessions in Schedule LXXX, decisions of the WCO may be relevant; and, therefore, they should have been examined by the Panel.

The above quoted passage did not decide the issue in definitive manner, but the door has certainly been opened. Note though, that as suggested above, it is simply not the case that all WTO members participate in the HS Committee, as a few have not signed it, even though they have de facto adhered to its disciplines. If HS Committee classifications are acknowledged the status of "subsequent practice", then a sub-set of the WTO membership through its actions will be in a position to influence the trade behavior of non-participating members.

But the HS Committee has very wide membership, and almost the totality of the WTO membership are members. This was, we can conclude, a calculated risk that the Appellate Body undertook when pronouncing on this score.

Note the difference between this case, and the discussion we entertained in Chapter 3 regarding Annex I(k) of the SCM Agreement: there are no statutory underpinnings supporting the relevance of a "subsequent undertaking" regarding the HS Treaty, never mind ad hoc decisions like the one that occupied the minds of the Appellate Body members in EC—Computer Equipment.

Was this report a willful departure from the previous ruling, which required WTO membership-wide harmonious practice for subsequent practice to exist in the first place? In a subsequent case, in EC—Chicken Cuts, the panel held that practice by even one WTO member alone can qualify as subsequent practice if it is the only relevant practice (§7.289). In the case at hand, the EU was the only importing WTO member with practice of classifying the products in question (salted chicken cuts). On appeal, the Appellate Body half-closed the door to this understanding of the term "subsequent practice", when it held that a few WTO members (but not only one) might establish subsequent practice, if only a few have traded in a particular commodity. The Appellate Body rejected the view that reliance on practice by just one member is relevant to establishing subsequent practice in the VCLT sense of the term (§254):

> We share the Panel's view that not each and every party must have engaged in a particular practice for it to qualify as a "common" and "concordant" practice. Nevertheless, practice by some, but *not all* parties is obviously not of the same order as practice by only one, or very few parties. To our mind, it would be difficult to establish a "concordant, common and discernible pattern" on the basis of acts or pronouncements of one, or very few parties to a multilateral treaty, such as the *WTO Agreement*. We acknowledge, however, that, if only some WTO Members have actually traded or classified products under a given heading, this circumstance may reduce the availability of such "acts and pronouncements" for purposes of determining the existence of "subsequent practice" within the meaning of Article 31(3)(b). (emphasis in the original)

In the same report, commenting on its prior report on EC—Computer Equipment, the Appellate Body noted (§260):

> The Appellate Body made these statements in the context of an interpretation pursuant to Article 32 of the *Vienna Convention*, but, as the Panel put it, these statements "confirm[] the importance of the classification practice of the importing Member whose schedule is being interpreted [but] also indicate[] that the classification practice of other WTO Members, including the exporting Member's practice, may be relevant." In our view, these statements cannot be read to justify exclusive reliance on the importing Member's classification practice. Therefore, we fail to see how the Panel's finding that it was "reasonable to rely upon EC classification practice alone in determining whether or not there is 'subsequent practice' that 'establishes the

agreement' of WTO Members within the meaning of Article 31(3)(b)" can be rec-
onciled with these statements of the Appellate Body in *EC—Computer Equipment*.
(emphasis in the original)

Consequently, a sub-set of the WTO membership might suffice for a finding
that subsequent practice exists, assuming one has not cherry-picked members
to pronounce in this manner. It seems that the Appellate Body, without saying
so, has veered towards evading sample bias. Whether this view will transpire
into subsequent agreements as well, remains to be seen in future practice.

1.2.4. Other relevant rules of public international law
The Appellate Body, in its report on EC—Chicken Cuts, held that the HS
treaty could also possibly qualify as an "other relevant rule of public international law" under Article 31.3(c) VCLT (§§195–200). Recall though that in the
same report the Appellate Body had classified the HS Treaty under "context".
The legal significance is the same, irrespective of whether the HS treaty qualifies as "context", or "other relevant rule of public international law": WTO
courts must take into account the HS treaty, as per the wording of Article 31
of the VCLT.

1.2.5. Special meaning
The panel on Mexico—Telecoms discussed at length (§§7.108–117) whether
the term "interconnection" appearing in the Telecoms Reference Paper had
been given a special meaning by the WTO negotiators, only to conclude that it
had not. In arriving at this conclusion, however, the panel neglected to review
carefully all the relevant negotiating documents. Indeed, some of them, such
as the Memorandum on Accounting Rates,[20] could have led the panel to conclude that the term "interconnection" was meant to cover only Mode 3, that is,
cases where an investor establishes commercial presence in a foreign country
and supplies services from its premises. The panel paid lip service to this and
similar documents, and ended up concluding that there was room for international interconnection under the WTO Agreement on Telecommunications.

1.2.6. Supplementary means of interpretation
The discussion so far has pointed to a handful of elements that have been classified under the various headings appearing in Article 31 of the VCLT. WTO

---

[20]   This memorandum is an understanding reached at the end of the negotiations and
reflected in paragraph 7 of the "Report of the Group on Basic Telecommunications",
WTO Doc. S/GBT/4 of February 15, 1997. The understanding was later confirmed by
the Council for Trade in Services, in paragraph 8 of the "Report to the General Council
on Activities During 1997", WTO Doc. S/C/5 of November 28, 1997.

adjudicating bodies on the other hand, have had recourse to dozens of other elements in order to interpret the covered agreements. They consistently qualified them as "supplementary sources of interpretation", almost always in order to confirm an interpretation they had already reached. Supplementary means emerge as the most extensive category of interpretative elements. A host of heterogenous elements appear under this category.

Recall that, because of the term "may" in Article 32 of VCLT, the WTO adjudicator has consistently held that it enjoys substantial discretion to move to elements beyond those appearing in Article 31 of VCLT.[21] There are of course, many good reasons arguing against recourse to the negotiating record:

- Not every WTO member has participated in negotiations;
- the negotiating history often points to no concrete outcome; or
- a provision might have acquired a whole new meaning over the years, and recourse to the negotiating record could resemble an atavistic excursion, a time warp that could lead to a non-functional, unworkable understanding of a term.

There are also good arguments in favor of recourse to the elements included in Article 32 of the VCLT:

- Recourse to the negotiating history helps to ensure that, by the end of the interpretative exercise, WTO adjudicating bodies will have respected their mandate under Article 3.2 of DSU, that is, they will not have undone the balance of rights and obligations as struck by the framers, as it often includes information regarding the scope of the contractual arrangement;
- the negotiating history very often contains information about both the rationale for the agreement, as well as the objectives sought through its negotiation;
- and it may further include information that did not appear in the final text, but which could explain the intended meaning of aggregate contractual language.

One might add, what is the harm of consistently visiting the negotiating record? It is not of course the case that recourse to the negotiating record, the most frequently used supplementary means of interpretation, is panacea. A very appropriate illustration is offered by the subject matter of US—Upland Cotton, a dispute between the US and Brazil. The heart of the dispute con-

---

[21] The Appellate Body has held in Japan—Alcoholic Beverages II, that there can be no doubt that Article 32 of the VCLT as well had attained the status of a rule of customary international law (p. 97).

cerned the understanding of the discipline imposed in Article 10.2 of the WTO Agreement on Agriculture, which reads:

> Members *undertake to work toward the development* of internationally agreed disciplines to govern the provision of export credits, export credit guarantees or insurance programmes and, after agreement on such disciplines, to provide export credits, export credit guarantees or insurance programmes only in conformity therewith. (emphasis added)

The panel, quite surprisingly as we have noted elsewhere,[22] held that export credits were already disciplined by the WTO Agreement on Agriculture. And not only that. It was so persuaded that it was right, because the language was so clear (the words "undertake to work toward …" notwithstanding), that it did not have to even look into the negotiating record. The text itself in its view, was all quite clear. The Appellate Body, the majority view anyway, shared this view, and so stated in §623 of the report:

> We agree with the Panel that the meaning of Article 10.2 is clear from the provision's text, in its context and in the light of the object and purpose of the Agreement on Agriculture, consistent with Article 31 of the Vienna Convention. The Panel did not think it necessary to resort to negotiating history for purposes of its interpretation of Article 10.2. Even if the negotiating history were relevant for our inquiry, we do not find that it supports the United States' position. This is because it does not indicate that the negotiators did not intend to discipline export credit guarantees, export credits and insurance programs at all. To the contrary, it shows that negotiators were aware of the need to impose disciplines on export credit guarantees, given their potential as a mechanism for subsidization and for circumvention of the export subsidy commitments under Article 9. Although the negotiating history reveals that the negotiators struggled with this issue, it does not indicate that the disagreement among them related to whether export credit guarantees, export credits and insurance programs were to be disciplined at all. In our view, the negotiating history suggests that the disagreement between the negotiators related to which kinds of specific disciplines were to apply to such measures. The fact that negotiators felt that internationally agreed disciplines were necessary for these three measures also suggests that the disciplines that currently exist in the Agreement on Agriculture must apply pending new disciplines because, otherwise, it would mean that subsidized export credit guarantees, export credits, and insurance programs could currently be extended without any limit or consequence.

But still, the majority did check on the negotiating record alright. So did the minority opinion, which appears in §§631 et seq. We quote §636 below, which

---

²² Petros C. Mavroidis. 2016. The Regulation of International Trade, volume 2, MIT Press: Cambridge, Massachusetts, pp. 588 et seq.

focuses on the heart of the disagreement across the members of the Appellate Body Division entrusted with the adjudication of this dispute:

> I also find support for my view in the negotiating history. Of course, care must be taken in relying on negotiating history and I do not wish to imply that resort to Article 32 of the Vienna Convention is strictly necessary in these circumstances. Nevertheless, as I read it this history confirms my view that at the end of the Uruguay Round, negotiators had not agreed to subject export credit guarantees, export credits and insurance programs provided in connection with agricultural goods to the disciplines of the Agreement on Agriculture or to any other disciplines that existed at that time. Article 10.2, in my view, was intended to reflect this outcome. At one point in the negotiations, there was a proposal for applying to agricultural products the disciplines in the Illustrative List of Export Subsidies annexed to the SCM Agreement. This proposal was dropped in the Draft Final Act in favour of an "undertak[ing] not to provide export credits, export credit guarantees or insurance programs otherwise than in conformity with internationally agreed disciplines", which in turn was replaced by the current version of Article 10.2. The previous version of Article 10.2 (in the Draft Final Act) reflected an immediate undertaking "not to provide export credit guarantees, export credits or insurance programs otherwise than in conformity with internationally agreed disciplines", whatever those may have been. In contrast, no immediate commitment is evident from the current version of Article 10.2, which instead calls for continued negotiations and for WTO Members to provide export credits, export credit guarantees or insurance programs only in conformity with internationally agreed disciplines after agreement on such disciplines. This suggests to me that the negotiators were aware of the need to impose disciplines on export credit guarantees, given their potential as a mechanism for circumvention, but they were unable to agree upon and identify the disciplines that were to apply to such measures until disciplines were developed in the future. Thus, in my view, the negotiating history supports an interpretation that Article 10.2 was inserted to commit WTO Members to continue negotiating on the disciplines that would apply, in the future, and that no disciplines would apply to such measures until such time as disciplines were internationally agreed upon.

Recourse, thus, to the negotiating history could still lead to disagreements, as judges might be asked, on occasion at least, to ... interpret it. But the argument in favor of proceedings this way anyway is: what is lost when recourse to the negotiating record is being made? If at all, interpreters will have additional ammunition in their quest for understanding what has been contracted.

In the majority of cases, recourse to supplementary means has been made to confirm an opinion reached. The panel reports on India—Quantitative Restrictions (§5.110) and Canada—Pharmaceutical Patents (§7.47) are very appropriate illustrations to this effect.

Very infrequently, panels moved to the preparatory work even before exhausting the elements appearing in Article 31 of the VCLT. In Canada— Pharmaceutical Patents (§7.29) the panel was called to interpret the term "limited exceptions" featured in Article 30 of TRIPs, and moved directly to the preparatory work of the TRIPs Agreement, instead of examining the term in accordance with the sequence specified in the VCLT. By the same token, in Korea—Procurement (§§7.74–83), the panel moved directly to the nego-tiating history of Korea's accession to the WTO Agreement on Government Procurement in order to satisfy itself as to the actual extent of the obliga-tions assumed by Korea. In Canada—Dairy, after holding that a notation in Canada's schedule of commitment was not clear on its face, the Appellate Body (§138) moved to the preparatory work in order to clarify the scope of Canada's engagement and only thereafter considered the sources identified in Article 31 VCLT.

These are very, very rare instances, indeed, and arguably they contravene the economy of the Vienna Convention system. In the overwhelming majority of the cases, WTO adjudicating bodies have followed the sequence established in Article 31 of the VCLT, and the Appellate Body report on US—Gambling is a paradigmatic case speaking to this point (§§197–212).

The Appellate Body has endorsed the view that there is no statutory exhaus-tive list of supplementary means of interpretation (EC—Chicken Cuts, §283). As they retain discretion to this effect, WTO courts have used a plethora of supplementary means, that we have classified under three headings:

- WTO documents;
- WTO members' practice; and
- International practice.

Even a brief perusal of case law leaves no one in doubt that panel and Appellate Body reports consistently refer to past case law. We have already discussed past case law and the relevance of precedent, separately.

Let us start with WTO documents.

Previous GATT Agreements: during the Tokyo Round, a series of agreements were signed (the so-called "Tokyo Round Codes"). Participation in those agreements was optional. Most of these agreements have been carried over into the Uruguay Round. The Uruguay Round Agreement on Anti-dumping, for example, succeeded the Tokyo Round Agreement on this score. Importantly, however, those two agreements (as well as many others carried over from one round to the other) are not identical. Very often new provisions have been added, and some provisions have been deleted.

At the Uruguay Round, participation in the agreements signed was not optional (with the exception of the so-called Annex 4 or "plurilateral agree-ments"). The overwhelming majority of the Tokyo Round Codes were trans-formed into multilateral agreements, since the prevailing view was that the Uruguay Round package should represent a "single undertaking": members should abide by the whole package, with few, very few indeed exceptions.[23] Because of their overlapping content, the Tokyo Round agreements have been consistently treated as supplementary means of interpretation. An illustration of this pattern can be seen in Argentina—Poultry Anti-dumping Duties, where the panel dealt with a dispute on the consistency of Argentina's measures with the Agreement on Anti-dumping. In order to confirm its interpretation of Article 2, the panel referred to the more explicit wording of the corresponding provision in the Tokyo Round Agreement (§7.358).

Negotiating Documents: in GATT/WTO practice, it is quite common for participating negotiators to ask the Chairman of a negotiating group to sum up in a paper the picture emerging from group discussions at a certain stage. Similar documents help reveal the extent of agreement, as well as the extent of disagreement among parties. But it is not only the Chairman that issues documents during this stage. Negotiating partners issue documents under their name, and the GATT/WTO Secretariat has been issuing documents (at the request of either the Chairman or the membership) as well. Sometimes even formal decisions are adopted at the negotiating stage, usually applied on provisional basis until a final decision on this matter has been adopted. Let us take them in turn, noting already that practice reveals that, as we climb the ladder from documents issued by trading nations to formal documents, their legal significance (and the ensuing persuasive power) increases. We will show that practice reveals that, who has issued the document, and following what process, matters.

The panel on US—Softwood Lumber III was dealing with a document which had been added to the Chairman's note, with the proviso that it was meant to facilitate discussions and in no way reflected the Chairman's views. When requested to provide an opinion on the legal relevance of this paper, the panel decided that it was of no probative value, largely because it was a document that did not reflect the Chairman's views and contained elements that aimed to "provoke" [sic] a discussion and thus, facilitate an agreement (§7.26).

This finding opened the door to acknowledging legal significance to Chair notes. Subsequent case law justified the expectations in this regard, drawing a distinction nevertheless, regarding their probative value.

---

[23]   Steinberg (2002) has claimed that the single undertaking was power-play whereby the US and the EU imposed their view on the rest of the world, whereas Wolfe (2009) has advocated, more persuasively we might add, the opposite opinion, see Richard H. Steinberg. 2002. In the Shadow of Law or Power? Consensus-Based Bargaining and Outcomes in the GATT/WTO, International Organization, 56: 339–374; and Robert Wolfe. 2009. The Single Undertaking as Negotiating technique and Constitutive Metaphor, Journal of International Economic Law, 12: 835 –858.

In US—Carbon Steel, the Appellate Body was dealing with a Chairman's note, and held that it could serve as indication as to what had been discussed among negotiators (§90). Footnote 83 to this paragraph is worth quoting:

> Having examined a number of proposals made by delegations, Notes by the Secretariat summarizing the discussions, and a succession of drafts of the Agreement, we are also unable to find any sign that this issue was addressed during the negotiations. (See, notably, the so-called "Cartland drafts" of 1990, MTN/GNG/ NG10/W/38 and Rev. 1, 2 and 3; and the "Dunkel Draft" of 1991, Draft Final Act Embodying the Results of the Uruguay Round of Multilateral Trade Negotiations, MTN.TNC/W/FA, 20 December 1991). Our review of certain commentaries on and summaries of the negotiation of the Anti-Dumping Agreement and the SCM Agreement – the negotiations of which were in part closely linked – also gives no indication that the issue arose during the negotiation.

In this paragraph, the Appellate Body reveals that, absence of mention in the various papers that the Chairman of the negotiating paper had issued, was fatal for an argument that an issue had been debated during negotiations. But what about the opposite scenario? What about cases where a disputing party claims that it has acted in accordance with what had been reflected in a Chairman's note?

The "Modalities Paper"[24] is a document prepared by the WTO Secretariat and circulated through the Chairman of the negotiating group on Agriculture. It reflects an agreement among negotiators during the Uruguay Round regarding the content of the schedules of commitments in farm trade. The Appellate Body on two occasions dismissed the interpretative relevance of the Modalities Paper altogether. In EC—Bananas III, it held that since it had not been explicitly referenced in the WTO Agreement on Agriculture, it was of little if any value (§157):

> We note further that the Agreement on Agriculture makes no reference to the Modalities document or to any "common understanding" among the negotiators of the Agreement on Agriculture that the market access commitments for agricultural products would not be subject to Article XIII of the GATT 1994.

In EC—Export Subsidies on Sugar, the Appellate Body adopted a more nuanced approach but did not deviate from its prior ruling either (§199):

> We do not find it necessary to decide in this appeal on the relevance of the "Modalities Paper". The "Modalities Paper" is not an agreement among the WTO Members and, by its terms, cannot be the basis of dispute settlement under the

---

[24]   Modalities for the Establishment of Specific Binding Commitments Under the Reform Programme, GATT Doc. MTN.GNG/MA/W/24 of December 20, 1993.

Marrakesh Agreement Establishing the World Trade Organization (the "WTO Agreement"). Furthermore, as the Appellate Body noted in EC – Bananas III, "the Agreement on Agriculture makes no reference to the Modalities document".

Now that is odd. The Modalities paper does not reflect partisan views, it was adopted by the Chairman, and served as basis for commitments entered. So, one might reasonably ask, what are the good arguments to neglect it other than formalism? Nothing it seems, as we explain later on. But let us first see how the document including scheduling modalities in the services sector was treated in case law.

In the GATS context, the panel on Mexico—Telecoms discussed, inter alia, the relevance of GATT/WTO Secretariat notes prepared at the request of the negotiating parties during a trade round. The Secretariat document was entitled "Scheduling of Initial Commitments in Trade in Services: Explanatory Note", a document that was later adopted by the GATS Council. The aim of the document, now widely known as the "Scheduling Guidelines", was to help WTO members with the scheduling of their commitments in the services sector. These guidelines are the GATS-equivalent to the GATT-relevant HS treaty.

In contrast to the HS treaty though, the Scheduling Guidelines were a decision by the GATS Council. The panel decided to use the guidelines as supplementary means (§§7.43–4). This finding was echoed in its report on US—Gambling (§§196-204), where the Appellate Body paid particular attention to the fact that WTO members had based their commitments on this document.

The Scheduling Guidelines and the Modalities Paper share an overlapping objective function. Under the circumstances, it seems that the rationale for accepting the Scheduling Guidelines as supplementary means, and rejecting the Modalities Paper, has to do with the form and process for adoption. The Modalities Paper is a document prepared by the WTO Secretariat and circulated through the Chairman of the negotiating group on Agriculture. Even though it has an official document number (MTN.GNG/MA/W/24), it is not a decision by a WTO organ. By contrast, the GATS Council formally adopted the Scheduling Guidelines.

Negotiating documents thus, in the form of Chairman's notes, have served as a basis to discard claims that an issue had been discussed and maybe even concluded. Conversely, they have served as benchmark to decide on the compliance of a member's behavior, only when they have reverted a certain form (e.g., through adoption following the GATT/WTO legislative process).

Informal Agreements Among WTO Members: in EC—Poultry, Brazil had argued that the bilateral "Oilseeds Agreement" that it had concluded with the EU was relevant to the dispute (§202). The Oilseeds Agreement had been negotiated within the framework of a re-negotiation of tariff commitments

(Article XXVIII GATT), and had been included in the modified schedule. Citing various precedents including the "Canada/EC—Wheat" arbitration in support, the panel decided that this document was decisive in determining the obligations that the EU had assumed vis-à-vis Brazil.

On appeal, the Appellate Body found that no reversible error in the panel's treatment of the Oilseeds Agreement had been committed. Accordingly, the Appellate Body stated that the Oilseeds Agreement may serve as a supplementary means of interpretation. Noting that the dispute concerned Schedule LXXX of the EU, and not the "Oilseeds Agreement", which was not a covered agreement (§81), the Appellate Body held that the latter had served as basis for the negotiation of the quota of Brazilian poultry to be imported in the EU, and hence could serve as supplementary means of interpretation (§83). The basis for this finding thus, was the link between the subject-matter of the "Oilseeds Agreement" with a covered agreement (Schedule LXXX, since all schedules are integral part of the GATT).

In subsequent case law, close connection between the subject matter of a bilateral agreement and a covered agreement emerges as the criterion for deciding whether a bilateral agreement would be taken into account by a WTO adjudicating body. In EC—Commercial Vessels, for example, the panel examined the content of a bilateral agreement between Korea and the EU (the so-called "Agreed Minutes"), in order to decide whether the EU TDM (Trade Defense Mechanism) was or was not a subsidy to counteract Korean subsidies in the shipyard sector (§§7.130 et seq.).

Circumstances Surrounding the Conclusion of the WTO Agreement: Article 32 of VCLT draws a wedge between *travaux préparatoires* and "circumstances of conclusion" of a treaty, a term which must be given thus, a distinct meaning. In Canada—Dairy, Canada had asserted that its concession was meant to be continuation of past practice, and should be read in this way. The Appellate Body, having reached the conclusion that Canada's schedule was not clear, decided to check the negotiating history of the concession.

When moving there, it first observed that, contrary to what had been the case with the EC—Brazil Oilseeds Agreement, there was no bilateral agreement between Canada and the United States (the parties in dispute). The absence of agreement did not, however, stop the Appellate Body from moving on to examine the circumstances surrounding the conclusion of the WTO Agreement. It referred to positions taken by the parties to the dispute on this score during the WTO panel proceedings. It eventually upheld Canada's claim, and rejected the US view that what had been agreed was a commitment on minimum access opportunities (which would have led to important practical ramifications). In the panel's view, non-contradicted statements made during the negotiation of the concession by the Canadian representative amounted to a tacit agreement between the parties in dispute.

It is probably wise to treat this report as an outlier, even though the Appellate Body was in fact endorsing the panel's findings in this respect, and thus both WTO adjudicating bodies were effectively in agreement on this score (§139). This is the only instance so far where the Appellate Body has accepted a tacit agreement as a circumstance surrounding the negotiation of a concession. The evidentiary burden surrounding similar instances should not be underestimated, and this feature in and of itself could lead cautious panelists to adopt a different course of action in future practice.

A more structured (and more comprehensive) discussion regarding the understanding of the "circumstances surrounding the conclusion (of the WTO Agreement)" took place during the proceedings that led to the Appellate Body report on EC—Chicken Cuts. In this case, the Appellate Body provided its understanding of the term in quite detailed manner. It began by noting the content of circumstances of conclusion that the panel itself had endorsed (§285):

> The Panel considered as "circumstances of conclusion" in this case the "historical background compris[ing] the collection of events, acts and other instruments that characterize the prevailing situation in the European Communities" at the time the tariff commitment under heading 02.10 of the EC Schedule was negotiated. Accordingly, the Panel decided to "consider EC law and the EC's classification practice during the Uruguay Round negotiations to the extent that they are relevant to the conclusion of the EC Schedule pursuant to Article 32."

It then, in §289, provided its understanding of the scope of the term "circumstances of conclusion":

> An "event, act or instrument" may be relevant as supplementary means of interpretation not only if it has actually influenced a specific aspect of the treaty text in the sense of a relationship of cause and effect; it may also qualify as a "circumstance of the conclusion" when it helps to discern what the common intentions of the parties were at the time of the conclusion with respect to the treaty or specific provision.

Not all circumstances of conclusion are relevant of course and, in the Appellate Body's view, the relevance of a particular circumstance should be established on objective factors and not subjective intent. In this vein, an adjudicator can include different elements, such as (§291):

> the type of event, document, or instrument and its legal nature; temporal relation of the circumstance to the conclusion of the treaty; actual knowledge or mere access to a published act or instrument; subject matter of the document, instrument, or event in relation to the treaty provision to be interpreted; and whether or how it was used or influenced the negotiations of the treaty.

The Appellate Body, in the same report, also dealt with the time-period that is relevant for discerning the (relevant) "circumstances of conclusion" (§293):

> Events, acts, and instruments may form part of the "historical background against which the treaty was negotiated", even when these circumstances predate the point in time when the treaty is concluded, but continue to influence or reflect the common intentions of the parties at the time of conclusion.

Knowledge about the instruments must exist. In the Appellate Body's view, this condition is met when a party has published and made it publicly available so that any interested party could be privy to information (§297).

This report is an outlier in a different sense. Even though, clearly, it reflects the Appellate Body's view of the manner in which "circumstances of conclusion" should be understood in WTO law, there is no other subsequent example where the Appellate Body (or a panel for that purpose) showed the same zest to delve into the negotiating record.

Note also that this report was issued on September 12, 2005. The report that discussed the Modalities of scheduling commitments in farm trade (EC—Export Subsidies on Sugar) had been issued on April 28, 2005. One Appellate Body member was present in both proceedings, and all remaining members participated in the discussions in both cases. How difficult was it to explain why the decision to deny any relevance to the Modalities document in EC—Export Subsidies on Sugar, fell short of the comprehensively-discussed understanding of circumstances of conclusion of the Agreement on Agriculture, as expressed in EC—Chicken Cuts? And yet, it did not happen. This is quite paradoxical, all the more so as form is not one of the criteria retained in the Appellate Body's analysis, when it comes to deciding what a relevant circumstance surrounding the conclusion is.

We can now move to discuss the relevance of the practice of WTO members.

Domestic Court Decisions Issued at the Time of Negotiation: the Panel on EC—Chicken Cuts took the view that domestic court decisions could be regarded as supplementary means of interpretation (§7.392). In the case at hand, Brazil had challenged the EU's unilateral decision to change the tariff treatment of salted chicken cuts (after the WTO Agreement was concluded) and subject them to a higher (than anticipated) tariff regime. The EU responded that its court decisions before the entry into force of the WTO Agreement made it clear that salted chicken cuts had consistently been subjected to the more burdensome of the relevant tariff categories. Although it eventually rejected the EU's claim, the panel accepted the relevance of similar decisions and reviewed them under the auspices of Article 32 VCLT.

On appeal, the Appellate Body confirmed the panel's understanding on this issue, adding that judgments will have less relevance than, for example, legislative acts, since they are, by definition, transaction-specific (§309):

> We share the Panel's consideration that judgments of domestic courts are not, in principle, excluded from consideration as "circumstances of the conclusion" of a treaty if they would be of assistance in ascertaining the common intentions of the parties for purposes of interpretation under Article 32. It is necessary to point out, however, that judgments deal basically with a specific dispute and have, by their very nature, less relevance than legislative acts of general application (although judgments may have some precedential effect in certain legal systems).

Domestic Law and Practice: pursuant to the VCLT (Article 27), domestic law cannot trump WTO law (a point explicitly acknowledged in the panel report in Argentina—Poultry Antidumping Duties, §7.108). This does not mean, however, that domestic law cannot provide a source of inspiration for WTO law.

In EC—Tariff Preferences, the panel (§7.11) examined the content of domestic codes of conduct for attorneys-at-law, focusing on issues such as the objectivity and independence of legal counsel, the right to consent to joint representation by the same counsel, and the equal right to discontinue such joint representation when conflicts potentially arise.

In EC—Computer Equipment, the Appellate Body held that the classification practice of the EU (the defendant in this case) was part of the circumstances surrounding the conclusion of the WTO Agreement (§§92–5). In the case at hand, the dispute between the United States and the EU concerned the latter's tariff treatment of some computer equipment.

In EC—Chicken Cuts, the Appellate Body added an important qualification. While acknowledging that the EU practice in this area was particularly relevant, the Appellate Body felt, as per our discussion above, that what ultimately mattered was the "prevailing internationally practice".

As the panel had pointed to a divergence of practice between the EU and the US, with regard to the classification of certain types of chicken, the panel had concluded that, its relevance notwithstanding, the EU practice was not dispositive of the issue of customs classification for these types of chicken (§§300 et seq.). In §307 of the same report, the Appellate Body concluded that there was no difference between this report and the report on EC—Computer Equipment, which should be read as a mere statement of relevance of a specific fact, and not as benchmark of what is and what is not a circumstance of conclusion (of a treaty). This statement had been included in §95 of its report on EC—Computer Equipment, but in the previous paragraph, the Appellate Body had noted (§94):

> If the classification practice of the importing Member at the time of the tariff nego-tiations is relevant in interpreting tariff concessions in a Member's Schedule, surely that Member's legislation on customs classification at that time is also relevant.

This paragraph, if read together with what came next, suggests that classification law and practice are relevant, and if consistent, all the more so. But the key question is this: they are relevant alright, but under which one of the elements of VCLT? The Appellate Body here as well did not respond, and if anything muddied the waters (once again).

We now move to discuss the relevance of international practice.

International Agreements: in the original and compliance reports on US—Shrimp, the Appellate Body referred to various regional and multilateral environmental agreements (MEAs), without classifying similar references as "other relevant rules of public international law". In its view, international agreements such as MEAs may not only be used as legal interpretation, but help to establish a wide agreement on certain facts (such as whether a species in endangered or whether certain resources are exhaustible), where such facts are pertinent to the application of a given legal provision.

As the Appellate Body itself explained in US—Shrimp (Article 21.5—Malaysia), the agreement is not thereby converted into an autonomous legal standard, but is merely evidence of non-comparable, and possibly discrimina-tory, treatment of non-signatories (§§124, 130).

The Appellate Body report on EC—Asbestos contains references to WHO (World Health Organization) conventions (§§124–35). Here, as in US—Shrimp cited above, the Appellate Body appears to have used these instru-ments as evidence of a wide agreement on a factual state of affairs, the toxicity of asbestos and its seriousness as a public health challenge.

UN Resolutions: the Arbitrator's report in US—FSC (Article 22.6—US) contains an explicit reference to the International Law Commission's (ILC) report on State Responsibility, although it did not specify what its legal value was (even though it saw it as support for the overall conclusions). The report, adopted as a resolution of the UN General Assembly, was intended to reflect customary international law. It has been referenced in various other reports ever since.

OECD Guidelines: the panel on Mexico—Telecoms relied on the OECD guidelines to confirm its understanding of the term "anti-competitive practice" (§7.236). In doing so, the Panel treated the OECD guidelines as supplementary means of interpretation. The same holds for the aforementioned references to OECD Guidelines in the panel on Argentina—Financial Services.

Decisions by International Courts: Occasionally, panels and the Appellate Body refer to decisions by other courts as means of supporting their own decisions. An appropriate illustration is India—Patents (US), where the Appellate Body referred to the jurisprudence of the Permanent Court of International Justice (PCIJ) to support its finding that the determination of domestic law should be treated as a factual matter (§65). In doing so, it did not clarify its legal status in WTO law. Nevertheless, it was arguably treating the PCIJ case law as supplementary means of interpretation.

Doctrine: sporadic references can be found in panel reports to the teachings and writings of highly qualified publicists, albeit rarely so. The quantity of references has picked up over the years, usually in a self-serving mood (that is, to support interpretations reached). Doctrine has always been used as supplementary means of interpretation.[25]

1.2.7.   Interpretative elements not mentioned in the VCLT

In interpreting the covered agreements, WTO courts have occasionally referred to *lex specialis*, which boils down to this: if two laws govern the same factual situation, a law governing it in more detail (*lex specialis*), takes precedence over a law governing it at an aggregate level (*lex generalis*).

This interpretative maxim was not explicitly included as such in the VCLT, but is consonant with the principle of "effective treaty interpretation" (*ut regis valeat quam paereat*), the cornerstone of the VCLT. By virtue of this maxim, the interpreter is called to ensure that terms will not be interpreted to redundancy as a result of extending the coverage of other terms. Were one not to start from the rule that specifically regulates a particular transaction[26] (and were to privilege, instead, the application of the more general rule), one risks making such specific rules redundant. In the words of the Appellate Body in US—Gasoline (p. 23): "An interpreter is not free to adopt a reading that would

---

[25]   This is not paradoxical, as the attitude of national courts towards doctrine is quite different even between courts belonging to the same legal family. Hynning (1956), among others, shows (pp. 129 et seq.) how US courts were traditionally more open towards doctrine than British courts, Christopher J. Hynning. 1956. Sources of International Law, Chicago-Kent Law Review, 34: 116–35.

[26]   Following EC—Asbestos, panels and the Appellate Body have, for example, consistently started their legal analysis of measures simultaneously falling under the ambit of both the GATT and the TBT Agreement (Technical Barriers to Trade) from the latter, that is, the agreement that more specifically regulates instruments such as "technical regulations" and "standards" which also come under the purview of the GATT, see, the panel reports on US—Clove Cigarettes, US—COOL, US—Tuna II (Mexico).

result in reducing whole clauses or paragraphs of a treaty to redundancy or inutility".[27]

The Appellate Body has also had recourse to the principle of "evolutionary interpretation" ("contemporaneity") in US—Shrimp. It had been asked to decide whether the term "exhaustible natural resources" appearing in Article XX(g) of GATT should be understood to cover living organisms as well, or simply non-living materials, as the negotiating history of Article XX(g) of GATT would have probably suggested (§130). This principle could in theory be likened to "subsequent practice" or even "subsequent agreement."[28] Citing a few international conventions and two GATT reports that had endorsed an expansive understanding of the term, the Appellate Body went on to decide in §131:

> Given the recent acknowledgement by the international community of the importance of concerted bilateral or multilateral action to protect living natural resources, and recalling the explicit recognition by WTO Members of the objective of sustainable development in the preamble of the WTO Agreement, we believe it is too late in the day to suppose that Article XX(g) of the GATT 1994 may be read as referring only to the conservation of exhaustible mineral or other non-living natural resources. Moreover, two adopted GATT 1947 panel reports previously found fish to be an "exhaustible natural resource" within the meaning of Article XX(g). We hold that, in line with the principle of effectiveness in treaty interpretation, measures to conserve exhaustible natural resources, whether living or non-living, may fall within Article XX(g).

This report raised a few issues. Subsequent practice/agreement in the VCLT sense of the term, can only refer to practice and/or agreement by the WTO members. Distefano (2011), in his authoritative study, looks into judicial practice and doctrine, and makes a clear link between the principle of contemporaneity and the relevant terms of VCLT (subsequent practice/agreement), which, of course, concerns exclusively the behavior of principals.[29] The Appellate Body provided no evidence to this effect, other than indirectly by referring to other international agreements, which some WTO members had signed, and some had not. Is that enough? No, of course not.

---

[27]   In this vein, the panel in its report in Canada—Patent Term tested whether the interpretation it reached on one TRIPs provision rendered redundant other related TRIPS pro-visions (§6.50).

[28]   Assuming of course that we are in presence of practice by the WTO Members, and not in presence of the judge's view with no empirical support to back it up.

[29]   Compare the thoughts of Friedmann, who calls for a specific comprehensive procedure to be followed, when courts move in and set aside anachronistic legal institutions, and fill in gaps, Wolfgang Friedmann. 1966. Limits of the Judicial Law-Making and Prospective Overruling, Modern Law Review: 29: 593–607.

Recall that a judge would be ill-advised to draw parallels with the OECD arrangement included in the SCM Agreement, which is a different story, as both the erstwhile as well as any successor agreement are explicitly referenced in the covered agreement. The HS treaty is also a different case, as all WTO members either de jure or de facto abide. The other element that the Appellate Body cited in support of its conclusion, is precedent to which we now turn.

1.3.　　The Inevitable Conclusion: Text First, Text Above All

What does our discussion above allow us to conclude? Recall, the overwhelming majority of interpretative elements used were classified as "supplementary means of interpretation". Recall further that, since panels have had recourse to similar elements overwhelmingly in order to confirm an interpretation that they had already derived by looking at the grammatical meaning of terms used, all these elements have hardly had any influence on the interpretations reached.

Were we thus to assign a co-efficient of relative importance, it is clear from WTO practice that classifying an element under Article 31 of the VCLT entails that this element will weigh in substantially more than another element that has been classified under Article 32 of the VCLT.

But only a handful of elements have been classified under the various headings of Article 31 VCLT. Our analysis confirms as much. The inevitable conclusion under the circumstances is that panels and the Appellate Body are textualist agents, interested primordially in the grammatical meanings of words used. They either presume that words reveal almost always the intention of negotiating parties, or they simply do not care about the intent. And they willfully ignore that the chosen words are a compromise between competing approaches, and thus most likely an imperfect signaling mechanism of contractual intentions, if analyzed in clinical isolation from the remaining elements appearing in Articles 31 and 32 of the VCLT.

Trachtman (1999) aptly called the Oxford Dictionary the source of law par excellence that the WTO had been using. This was not undeserved at all, as, especially the Appellate Body members have emerged as wordsmiths of the highest order. Indeed, Claus-Dieter Ehlermann, a former Appellate Body member admitted as much:

> [T]he Appellate Body has certainly attached the greatest weight to the first [term mentioned in Article 31 of the VCLT], i.e., "the ordinary meaning of the terms of the treaty." This is easily illustrated by the frequent references in Appellate Body

reports to dictionaries, in particular to the Shorter Oxford Dictionary, which, in the words of certain critical observers, has become "one of the covered agreements."[30]

Between an endless, finicky overlapping of paragraphs, and an anthology of pernickety repetitions of the same concept, in an ever-increasing list of reports cautioning panels that they misconstrued what the Appellate Body itself had pertinently suggested, the Appellate Body emerged as one of the most misunderstood courts in the world, when its words had been ... so clear.

And there is almost explicit admission to this effect. In US—Shrimp, the Appellate Body noted that there is a hierarchy across the various elements embedded in Article 31 of VCLT, noting that recourse to the object and purpose of the treaty is legitimate, only when recourse to the elements mentioned before in the body of Article 31 of VCLT has not helped the judges to reach a decision (§114):

> A treaty interpreter must begin with, and focus upon, the text of the particular provision to be interpreted. It is in the words constituting that provision, read in their context, that the object and purpose of the states parties to the treaty must first be sought. Where the meaning imparted by the text itself is equivocal or inconclusive, or where confirmation of the correctness of the reading of the text itself is desired, light from the object and purpose of the treaty as a whole may usefully be sought.

This view, we submit, is wrong. Both Jimenez de Arechaga (1978),[31] who participated in the negotiations of the VCLT, as well as the cited work by Wetzel and Rauschning (1978) confirm that the drafters included the general rule of interpretation in one sentence in order to avoid over- and/or under-emphasizing any one of the elements mentioned therein. It could be that the Appellate Body wanted to downplay teleological interpretations, where what matters is the ends sought irrespective of means committed. This is correct, as the means committed to achieve the ends (trade liberalization) matter. Panels cannot add to the obligations assumed, as per the oft-cited Article 3.2 of DSU. If this was the intention of the Appellate Body indeed, then this paragraph will go down in history as sloppy shorthand.

Trachtman's reaction mentioned above is largely justified by the extensive use of dictionaries, and more specifically the "Oxford English Dictionary", that panels and the Appellate Body have made. Words however, are not

---

[30]   Claus-Dieter Ehlermann. 2002. Six Years on the Bench of the "World Trade Court": Some Personal Experiences as a Member of the Appellate Body of the World Trade Organization, Journal of World Trade, 36: 605–39, at p. 638.

[31]   Eduardo Jimenez de Arréchaga. 1978. International Law in the Past Third of the Century, Recueil des Cours, 159. The Hague: Brill Academic Publishers.

invariances, and the context matters. As Orwell (1946) wrote: "let the meaning choose the word, and not the other way around".[32]

This can happen only if context has been accounted for, for words, especially in a negotiating context, serve an objective that negotiators want to achieve. The Appellate Body seemed to have gotten it right in its report on US—Gambling, when it stated that equating dictionary definitions to the ordinary meaning of terms is too mechanical an approach (§166). Alas, it did not always stick to these wise words in subsequent practice.

---

[32] George Orwell. 1946. Politics and the English Language, Penguin: London, United Kingdom.

7. Practice … and its discontents

1. A CRITICAL EVALUATION OF WTO COURTS' UNDERSTANDING OF SOURCES OF LAW

The discussion so far reveals that, while there should be no doubt as to what the WTO sources of law are, the haphazard recourse to VCLT has been a source of concern. The response to the question "has VCLT been properly used?" cannot be in the affirmative, and we have provided a lot of evidence to this effect.

Recall that the VCLT is a codification of customary rule, it is the distilled common denominator that is most acceptable to all parties. It seems to us that it is a stretch to argue that the fault (assuming there is fault) lies with the VCLT per se. The VCLT is no stairway to institutional imbalances. It must be the use that WTO courts have made of the VCLT that is the source of discontent. For it is quite clear that discontent exists. In a recent survey conducted among stakeholders,[1] a number of them expressed concerns regarding the quality of the output by WTO courts, even though no one was prepared to take drastic measures to redress the situation, like the Trump Administration did. The quality of output is to a large extent a function of the manner in which WTO courts have understood the VCLT-regime. There are of course other contributing factors as well.

One way to graphically represent our discussion regarding the use of VCLT, is this:

	False Positives	False Negatives
Extensive Margin	a	b
Intensive Margin	c	d

- (a) refers to instances like the treatment of *amicus* briefs, and other non-functional innovations, some of which have been acquiesced to by the membership (and we will be discussing them in the following pages);

---

[1] Matteo Fiorini, Bernard M. Hoekman, Petros C. Mavroidis, Maarja Saluste and Robert Wolfe. 2020. WTO Dispute Settlement and the Appellate Body Crisis: Insider Perceptions and Members' Revealed Preferences, Journal of World Trade, 54: 667–98.

- (b) could encompass instances like the treatment of the Modalities document, and in more general terms of the negotiating record;
- (c) and (d) could cover cases like the principle of "contemporaneity" invoked in US—Shrimp, but also the differentiated treatment of the Modalities document when compared to the treatment afforded to the GATS Scheduling Guidelines.

The overall attitude of the WTO courts has not helped. WTO courts, as we explain, and especially the Appellate Body, will not refrain from exercising jurisdiction, except in the extreme case where disputing parties have requested to do so. But let us take first a more detailed look into the nature of the agency contract between the WTO members and the WTO adjudicators.

1.1.   The Nature of the Contract Between the WTO Membership and WTO Adjudicators

Recall that the WTO DSU has adopted a two-tier system with respect to the selection of judges: direct appointments by the principals as far as the Appellate Body members are concerned, and indirect (sometimes) appointments through the Secretariat, when it comes to panel members.

In fact, the WTO Members have empowered the WTO Secretariat with substantial discretion in the appointment of WTO adjudicators at the panel stage: it can propose individuals anyway (Article 8.6 DSU), and it can even appoint them to adjudicate, if members cannot agree to the proposed individuals, and a request to this effect has been tabled (Article 8.7 DSU). In practice, the Secretariat has appointed at least one panelist in 70 percent of all panels, the percentage being closer to 80 percent for the second half of all panels established. 66 percent of all appointed panelists are non-roster, that is, they have not been proposed by the membership, but instead have been selected by the Secretariat. In fact, 429/650 panelists appointed so far are non-roster.[2] The members of the Appellate Body are selected directly by the membership.

There is of course, nothing new in establishing some sort of "double agency" in the WTO: shareholders often mandate a Board to appoint the company's executive organs. By empowering the Secretariat as discussed above, transactions costs were mitigated (since the membership did not have to appoint directly both bodies, panels and the Appellate Body). Since the collective will, at the time at least, was to have ad hoc panels (and not something

---

[2]   When expressed in time-series, the number of non-roster is higher in the second, more recent of all disputes submitted so far. In Mavroidis (2022), we show that in the last ten years (2010–20), we observe more Secretariat appointees, and more non-roster panelists appointed as well, see Mavroidis (2022).

akin to a first instance adjudicating body with permanent composition), similar costs should not be under-estimated as litigating parties would have to agree on three panelists roughly 24 times a year.[3] Furthermore, appointing ad hoc panelists had worked quite well during the GATT era (1947–94), as Hudec (1993) has shown. Naturally then, the WTO framers did not want to undo a winning formula.

But this decision comes at a cost. The cost is that, since three different actors are implicated in the process (membership, Secretariat, adjudicators), they risk having different preferences. The risk for adverse selection and/or moral hazard cannot be excluded out of hand. Maybe this cost was mitigated during the GATT years because of the relative homogeneity of the membership, which had promoted a culture of cooperation that transpired into the later years as well, when the membership's homogeneity was being diluted. The WTO membership is definitely a different world.

We are dealing here with a multiple principal problem (common agency), as the two agents (Secretariat, adjudicators) are called to serve 164 masters.[4] The increasing heterogeneity of the membership entails also increasing heterogeneity of preferences across the principals.

Assume there is no Secretariat, and that members choose their adjudicators directly (incurring thus the marginal transaction costs). Assume a litigation between Home and Foreign, two WTO members. We are now squarely within a multiple-principal scenario, where, except for asymmetric information between principals and agents (adjudicators), there could be asymmetric information across the two principals as well. The fact that the total number of WTO members is 164 exacerbates the size of the problem. Now what kind of issues can arise in this context?

For starters, Home and Foreign could be vying to influence their common agent (the adjudicator) in order to secure a favorable to them result. The consequences could be detrimental to the regime as such, as Home (or Foreign)

---

[3]   In Mavroidis (2022), we provide the overall numbers of disputes for each year since 1995.

[4]   Alter (2008) makes a very persuasive argument to the effect that, in international adjudication, it is a quixotic test to re-write the contract in such a way, so as to reduce (and hopefully eliminate) the discretion of agents (judges). We subscribe to this conclusion, even though Alter refuses to call international judges agents, and prefers the term "trustees" for reasons that she explains in her paper. The key element of her analysis is that there is (potentially) an issue, which is hard to address, namely reduce drastically/ eliminate judicial discretion in international adjudication, see Karen J. Alter. 2008. Agents or Trustees? International Courts in their Political Context, European Journal of International Relations, 14: 33–63.

might be prepared to lobby the agent to secure a positive outcome:[5] assuming the common agent succumbs to a partisan view, the law will (most likely) be misinterpreted creating, besides a dangerous precedent, skepticism among the membership regarding the trustworthiness of the adjudication branch of the WTO.

But there is more. Since the WTO counts 164 members, we could be facing a collective action problem, as some members might prefer to free-ride on others' efforts to perform surveillance of the behavior of the adjudicators.[6] One would expect those WTO members who combine fewer litigation and scarce administrative resources to do so. Adjudicators could thus rationally "shirk" (relatively) safe in the knowledge that their actions will remain un-observed. The opposite could also be true, as we could be observing over-zealous monitoring by those possessing the means to do so, which could lead to duplication, and further discouragement to monitor the behavior of agents.[7] The consequence is more leeway for the agents and probably more "shirking".

A different issue could arise though, which could irk principals, even when adjudicators have performed their tasks as they should, as WTO adjudicators will be called to interpret one incomplete contract (WTO) through another (VCLT), and the preferences of principals and agents regarding what has been included in and/or omitted from the contract might differ.

The underlying assumption is, of course, that by adhering to the VCLT, the balance of rights and obligations (the common intent of the parties) will not be undone, otherwise Article 3.2 of the DSU makes no sense.[8] But the question is of course, whether this underlying assumption is correct at all. Instead of re-inventing the wheel, we can start empirically, looking into the sample of cases where either WTO adjudicators ended up with irreconcilable interpretations of the same provision, and/or into the "*cahier des doléances*" that the US delegation recently submitted,[9] or even at previous grievances that WTO

---

[5]   B. Douglas Bernheim, and Michael D. Whinston. 1986. Common Agency, Econometrica, 54: 923–42.

[6]   Sean Gailmard. 2009. Multiple Principals and Oversight of Bureaucratic Policy-Making, Journal of Theoretical Politics, 21: 161–86.

[7]   Fahad Khalil, David Martimort, and Bruno Parigi. 2007. Monitoring a Common Agent: Implications for Financial Contracting, Journal of Economic Theory, 135: 35–67.

[8]   To avoid misconceptions, we are interested in the relationship between the membership and its agents, and not in the hierarchical relationship between panels and the Appellate Body, which can hardly be viewed from a principal-agent angle for the reasons developed in Jonathan Remy Nash and Rafael I. Pardo. 2013. Re-thinking the Principal-Agent Theory of Judging, Iowa Law Review, 99: 331–62.

[9]   USTR. 2020. Report on the Functioning of the Appellate Body of the World Trade Organization, USTR: Washington D.C., available at https://ustr.gov/sites/default/files/enforcement/DS/USTR.Appellate.Body.Rpt.Feb2020.pdf.

members have voiced. Inconsistent case law, by definition, cannot satisfy the common intent, for the common intent cannot have been to serve one sauce for the goose and another for the gander.

This is, of course, partly the case because, as Horn, Maggi and Staiger (2010) have persuasively argued,[10] the WTO contract is an "obligationally" incomplete contract. The more room a contract leaves for discretion, the higher the likelihood that not everyone will be happy with the manner in which the appointed agents have exercised discretion. Some will be happy, and some not, and cases of collective unhappiness are very, very rare indeed. Alter (2008) is hence absolutely right when arguing that, unlike other cases, in the realm of international adjudication (à la WTO) it is far from evident how principals can re-contract so as to eliminate the potential for moral hazard.

The VCLT, when viewed in this perspective, is an aggravating factor. It contains various elements that the judge must take into account when interpreting a legal canon. The cogent, coherent with the legislative intent, understanding of the VCLT is to view it as a whole, and the choice of lumping all interpretative elements in one sentence reflects precisely this understanding.[11] In the hands of the WTO judge, it has become a whole divided into parts, with textual interpretations being the dominant element, whereas all other elements are reduced to supporting act (confirmation of textual interpretations).[12] Ideally, one would like to see a return to "orthodoxy"; a second-best could be some sort of understanding (a co-efficient) regarding the relative importance of

---

[10]   Henrik Horn, Giovanni Maggi and Robert W. Staiger. 2010. Trade Agreements as Endogenously Incomplete Contracts, American Economic Review, 100: 394–419.

[11]   Both Jimenez de Arréchaga, a negotiator of the VCLT, as well as Wetzel and Rauschning, who provided the definitive account of the negotiation of the agreement, have concluded in this way, see Jimenez de Arréchaga (1978), and Wetzel and Rauschning (1978) op. cit.

[12]   The universal (in the realm of international law) prevalence of the VCLT is predicated on the comprehensive list of elements that the interpreter must employ in order to perform an exegesis of the legal canon it has been called to interpret. Some domestic legal systems have adopted a less hands-on approach, and have not imposed an inquiry into specific elements in order to decide the scope and meaning of a rule. For example, a few Civil Codes in Continental Europe, request from judges to detect the "intent" of the contracting parties, without enumerating one-by-one the VCLT elements. Understanding the "intent" involves some sort of inquiry into the economy of the contractual arrangement, a systematic reading which will eliminate inconsistencies and redundancies. This is also the objective of VCLT, embedded in the Latin maxim *ut regis valeat quam pereat* (literally, it is better for a rule to have a meaning than be void thereof), referred to as "the principle of effective interpretation" which requests from judges to avoid over- or under-interpreting specific provisions. Alas, in the name of sequentially, and in compartmentalized manner, going through the various VCLT elements one by one, the WTO judge has often sacrificed the overarching objective.

each element. In the absence thereof, panels have used the leeway provided by the VCLT, to reach conclusions which are hard to reconcile on even the foundational terms of the WTO contract. Think of "like" goods in DS8 (Japan—Taxes on Alcoholic Beverages) and DS135 (EC—Asbestos), or the back and forth in the zeroing disputes, etc.[13] Examples abound, and we will provide a few more in the next chapter.

The long and the short of this discussion is that, even assuming that principals arrive through intense efforts to as close as possible a "complete" contract, recourse to the VCLT could still provide adjudicators with leeway and discretion.

And of course, the Secretariat is another complicating factor. Except for assisting in selecting adjudicators, the Secretariat as per Article 27.1 of DSU: "The Secretariat shall have the responsibility of assisting panels, especially on the legal, historical and procedural aspects of the matters dealt with, and of providing secretarial and technical support".

Members (principals) do not see eye to eye on a host of historical, legal issues, otherwise there would have been no disputes in the first place. Any opinion offered by the Secretariat on this score, by definition will not satisfy the totality of the membership. In this vein, attempts by the members to influence the Secretariat views (which could be lobbied to this effect) could, as argued already, lead to sub-optimal results. Depending on the quality of adjudicators (the amount of expertise they possess), the views of the Secretariat can weigh more or less in the final decision.[14] This is of course not a WTO idiosyncratic element, as recent research in other contexts reveals similar attitudes by Secretariat-type bodies with a say in adjudication.[15] And of course, adjudicators to the extent they find it worth it to repeat the experience and seek re-appointment, would rather align their views to those of the Secretariat, the organ entrusted with proposing (and, eventually, appointing) adjudicators.

But even if the Secretariat is always immune to pressures, and this is the key point, it will also use the VCLT to provide its views on what is right and what

---

[13] Thomas J. Prusa and Edwin Vermulst. 2009. A One-Two Punch on Zeroing: U.S.—Zeroing (EC) and U.S.—Zeroing (Japan), World Trade Review, 8: 187–241.

[14] In an often-cited account, the late Chief Justice William Rehnquist had argued that it does not matter who holds the pen, what matters is who ultimately decides, see William H. Rehnquist. 1957. Who Writes Decisions of the Supreme Court? U.S. News & World Report, December 13, 74. The problem is that, unlike the US Supreme Court Justices, many panelists do not possess the requisite knowledge (and sometimes even lack the incentives) to refute legal opinions advanced by members of the WTO Secretariat.

[15] Peter Mascini and Nina L. Holvast. 2020. Explaining Judicial Assistants' Influence on Adjudication with Principal–Agent Theory and Contextual Factors. International Journal for Court Administration, 11: 5–23.

is wrong. It cannot do otherwise, as its role is to assist adjudicators who must use VCLT, as per the consistent understanding of the reference to "customary rules of interpretation of public international law" embedded in Article 3.2 of DSU.

To be sure, no WTO member and/or adjudicator has openly accused the WTO Secretariat of unduly trying to influence the views of those entrusted with the decision-making at the adjudication stage. There are voices to this effect that originate in other tribunals, and we have observed sometimes virulent attacks against members of an international secretariat that attempted to influence the outcome of arbitral tribunals. Professor Jan Dalhuisen, one of the appointed arbitrators in an investment-dispute, openly blamed members of the International Center for the Settlement of Investment Disputes (ICSID) Secretariat, for attempting to steer the panel towards a particular outcome.[16]

What we have in a few instances observed in the WTO, is the expression of some members' disappointment with the manner in which the WTO Secretariat has selected members of panels. In Mavroidis (2022), quoting from WTO public documents (the Minutes of the Dispute Settlement Body, DSB) we have provided a list of the cases where members have criticized Secretariat appointments to panels.

The conclusion from this discussion is two-fold:

- The agency (and, on occasion, double agency) embedded in the DSU selection process for adjudicators, can lead to distortions;
- recourse to the VCLT makes it a quixotic test to even attempt to write a contract that will significantly reduce judicial discretion by WTO adjudicators. Some improvements are possible, and we will include some proposals in favor of introducing indicative lists in law-making that help minimize type II errors (false negatives), but the VCLT inherently carries within it judicial discretion regarding the interpretation of law that cannot be eliminated through additional law-making.

The attitude of WTO adjudicators has increased the volume of concerns, as they have refused to shy away, even when they could have legitimately done so, from exercising their duties. We turn to this issue in what now follows.

---

[16] Available at https://jusmundi.com/en/document/opinion/pdf/en-compania-de -aguas-del-aconquija-s-a-and-vivendi-universal-s-a-formerly-compania-de-aguas-del -aconquija-s-a-and-compagnie-generale-des-eaux-v-argentine-republic-i-additional -opinion-of-professor-jh-dalhuisen-.

1.2. The Extreme Anxiety to Avoid Committing a False Negative

WTO courts have never shied away from their tasks. In fact, they have not refused jurisdiction, even when the better arguments lied with denying it. The larger the pie of course, the likelier the probability to err. WTO courts were not deterred.

1.2.1. Jurisdiction declined

WTO courts, like any court and/or arbitral tribunal, have the right to decide whether they are competent to adjudicate a dispute (Kompetenz Kompetenz). They have rarely if ever refrained from exercising jurisdiction. The DSU prejudges their discretion of course in one instance: Article 12.12 states that a panel's authority has lapsed if, twelve months after it had been requested to stay proceedings, no request to reconvene has been submitted. And we know that panels have espoused *res judicata*, and some panels the estoppel principle as well (even though the Appellate Body has narrowed its relevance to almost redundancy), which also restrain panels' jurisdiction.

Panels have further declined jurisdiction, observing the parties' wish to this effect. In Brazil—Aircraft (Article 22.6—Brazil), the panel noted that an agreement had been concluded between the two parties not to seek countermeasures pending the report by the compliance panel. In its view, this agreement was binding on the parties to the dispute, and it did not include any findings on this issue (§3.8). In India—Autos, the panel explained the conditions under which a mutually agreed solution restrains its jurisdiction (§§7.116–24).

Panels have also refrained from entertaining claims that were not presented before the establishment of the panel, during the stage of consultations (Appellate Body report on US—Certain EC Products, at §70). This is a principle well-embedded in the multilateral legal order since the GATT days. The only genuine innovation in this context has to do with timely submission of claims. In US—Carbon Steel, the Appellate Body confirmed the panel's decision to reject a claim by the US which was first presented at the interim review stage, since it was running counter to due process considerations, even though it did not exclude the possibility that other jurisdictional claims, unrelated to the terms of reference (as was this one), could be raised at any stage during the proceedings (§123).

1.2.2. The political question doctrine in WTO law

On its way to constructing the scaffolding for future disputes dealing with national security, in footnote 183 (to §7.103) of its report on Russia—Traffic in Transit, the panel rejected an argument advanced by Russia to the effect that national security is a political question that should remain non-justiciable:

> The ICJ has rejected the "political question" argument, concluding that, as long as the case before it or the request for an advisory opinion turns on a legal question capable of a legal answer, it is duty-bound to take jurisdiction over it, regardless of the political background or the other political facets of the issue … Moreover, the Panel notes that in Mexico—Taxes on Soft Drinks, the Appellate Body expressed the view that a panel's decision to decline to exercise validly established jurisdiction would not be consistent with its obligations under Articles 3.2 and 19.2 of the DSU, or the right of a Member to seek redress of a violation of obligations within the meaning of Article 23 of the DSU.

Now, there is little doubt that the second ground for declining the Russian request is correct. But the former is of doubtful validity in the WTO context. For starters, the sources of law of the ICJ and the WTO are not identical, as WTO courts have a much narrower pool of sources to draw from, as we have already explained. But, more generally, why would the ICJ attitude bind WTO panels? It seems that the panel made a leap of faith here.

In a subsequent case, involving the alleged violation of intellectual property rights (Saudi Arabia—Intellectual Property Rights), this issue resurfaced. This time, the panel borrowed from Russia—Traffic in Transit, and in §§7.16–7.17, it explicitly denied the Saudi request to reject the claim, because the dispute was "political", and thus, the panel could not resolve it in the first place. We quote:

> The Panel is not persuaded that it can decline to make any findings or a recommendation, i.e. "decline to exercise its jurisdiction" on the basis of Saudi Arabia's argument that the "real dispute" between the parties is not a "trade dispute". The Panel considers that it is evident from its terms of reference that it has not been asked by Qatar or the DSB to make any findings or recommendation on any wider dispute between the parties. The matter raised by Qatar in its panel request, which now forms the Panel's terms of reference, concerns alleged violations of the TRIPS Agreement. Accordingly, the matter before the Panel falls within the legal subject-matter jurisdiction of a WTO dispute settlement panel.
> For similar reasons, the Panel is not persuaded that it can decline to exercise jurisdiction on the basis of Saudi Arabia's argument that it is impossible for any findings or recommendation to secure a positive solution to "the matter" and/or achieve a satisfactory settlement of "the dispute" under the DSU. The Panel considers that this argument, like Saudi Arabia's argument concerning the "real dispute" not being a "trade dispute", is directed at the wider political dispute between the parties that is not at issue before the Panel. The Panel recalls that Article 3.4 of the DSU provides that recommendations or rulings made by the DSB are to be aimed at achieving a "satisfactory settlement of the matter in accordance with the rights and obligations under [the DSU] and under the covered agreements". The Panel considers that the "matter" referred to in Article 3.4 is the "matter referred to the DSB" by a complainant in its panel request, as provided under Article 7.1 of the DSU. Thus, in this

dispute, the matter for which a satisfactory settlement is to be achieved is the "matter referred to the DSB" by Qatar in its panel request, which, in turn, circumscribes the Panel's terms of reference. The Panel is therefore not persuaded by Saudi Arabia's arguments under Articles 3.7 and 11 of the DSU.

Two panel reports thus have by now endorsed the view that there is no room for the "political question" doctrine in the WTO. This is an issue that has been hotly debated in various contexts. The ICJ reaction mentioned above is quite typical. The CJEU as well has not explicitly admitted to the relevance of the doctrine even though, as Butler (2018) has argued,[17] one can encounter some aspects of the doctrine in case law.

The political question doctrine comes quite close to the idea of justiciability, and the ensuing question is whether courts are the appropriate forum to hear a given case. The question more precisely is whether an issue can appropriately be put forward before a judicial body, or, because of its nature, it should better be handled by a different body? The answer might be straight forward if there is an explicit statement regarding the non-justiciability of a clause. But what if a statement to this effect is missing? Should courts go ahead anyway, or refrain from adjudicating?

This question has divided scholars and judicial bodies. In the US for example, starting with *Baker v. Carr*,[18] the US Supreme Court concluded that the political question doctrine did not bar courts from reaching the merits of a challenge brought against Tennessee's system of apportioning its state legislature, even though the case was about politics. More recently, in *Rucho v. Common Cause*,[19] the same Court, by a vote of five to four, concluded that no judicially manageable standards existed for distinguishing between routine and extreme gerrymandering, that could be applied by the federal courts. The academia is equally divided. There are sceptics like Henkin (1976),[20] who wondered whether there is a downside if courts were pro-active, and Barkow (2002),[21] who fears that neglect of the doctrine could lead to over-judicialization of public life.

In the WTO context, the question would be whether all of the rights and obligations included in the covered agreements are justiciable. Courts will have to decide whether, because of Article 3.2 of the DSU, they are obliged to

---

[17]   Graham Butler. 2018. In Search of the Political Question Doctrine in EU Law, Legal Issues of Economic Integration, 45: 329–54.

[18]   369 US 186 (1962).

[19]   No 18-422, 588 US _ (2019).

[20]   Louis Henkin. 1976. Is There a Political Question Doctrine? Yale Law Journal, 85: 597–625.

[21]   Rachel Barkow. 2002. More Supreme Court? The Fall of the Political Question Doctrine, and the Rise of Judicial Supremacy, Columbia Law Review, 102: 237–336.

review disputes submitted to them to the extent, of course, that the facts have been appropriately subjected to a specific provision of a covered agreement. So far, panels based on Article 3.2 of DSU, have rejected claims that they should decline their jurisdiction because of the nature of the disputed provision. The question of standard of review is a sequential question: it does not arise, unless a court has jurisdiction to adjudicate a dispute.

1.2.3.   Institutional balance

The political question doctrine (as presented in WTO adjudication) is related to, but does not overlap with, the question of institutional balance, which has been discussed in the WTO. A claim that institutional balance has been altered, presupposes that a particular issue has been entrusted to a non-judicial body.

The panel in Turkey—Textiles dealt with the issue whether a TMB (Textiles Monitoring Body) decision binds a panel, which is subsequently called to deal with it. It held that panels are not bound by TMB decisions, and can decide an issue independently of the content of a prior TMB decision (§8.92). In the context of the same dispute, the issue arose whether panels should be reviewing the consistency of an FTA/CU (customs union) with the WTO rules. The argument advanced by the respondent (Turkey) was that this could not be the case since the consistency of an FTA/CU with the multilateral rules came exclusively under the purview of the CRTA (Committee on Regional Trade Agreements), the WTO organ that would be notified of all FTAs/CUs, and where discussions about their consistency with the WTO rules could be raised. In Turkey's view, panels should refrain from addressing such issues until the CRTA has issued its final report. The panel rejected this argument.

This issue was discussed again by a subsequent panel, dealing with India—Quantitative Restrictions (§§5.93–4). India[22] had imposed a quantitative restriction which it was trying to justify through recourse to the BOP (Balance of Payments) Committee. At the time of the establishment of the panel, the BOP Committee had not reached any decision on the issue. The panel first explained that, assuming it had ruled first (e.g., before the BOP Committee had done so) on the issue, nothing would prevent the BOP Committee from reaching a different conclusion on the same issue; conversely, in case the BOP Committee had already decided the issue, it could see no reason why it would not take the conclusions reached into account. On appeal, the Appellate Body upheld this finding (§§99 and 105).

---

[22]   Ironically, India was involved in both cases, and argued once in favor of extending the panel's jurisdiction to cover issues also entrusted to WTO Committees, and once against similar extension.

The inescapable conclusion is that panels will not shy away from their tasks. They have not admitted the relevance of the political question doctrine, and they do not see how institutional balance could lead to an evisceration of their tasks. The WTO courts have not shied away from their duties insisting on a literal understanding of Article 3.2 of the DSU, which they understand as obliging them to adjudicate, and not as merely circumscribing the sources of WTO law, without prejudging their justiciability.

There are some refreshing, dare we say, illustrations to the opposite. In US—Softwood Lumber IV, the panel had been called to examine the USDOC (US Department of Commerce) calculation of the benefit conferred on the softwood lumber producers by the Canadian government.[23] Let us go through the facts of this case first.

The US, when calculating the amount of subsidy that Canadian producers of softwood lumber had received, had used US instead of Canadian prices as benchmark. The reason for doing so, in the US view, was that none of the benchmarks mentioned in the body of Article 14 of SCM was reasonable. The US had claimed before the panel, that it would have been meaningless anyway to have used Article 14(d) of SCM as benchmark for the calculation of benefit (which refers to the "prevailing market conditions" in the subsidizing country), since there were no market conditions at all prevailing in Canada with respect to the lumber market: the price of land had been heavily subsidized almost throughout the Canadian territory, leaving no room for market forces to establish a price. The price in the few private lands would necessarily follow the government price. Under the circumstances, an appropriate benchmark (counterfactual) for calculating the amount of benefit received by the government was missing. The amount of benefit, in the US view, could never be calculated by comparing two non-market prices.

The panel disagreed with the approach, even though it had some sympathy for the spirit permeating the argument. In its reading of Article 14, there was no room for using out of country benchmarks. The panel's analysis was based on the language of Article 14 of SCM (§7.45 of the report). It concluded that (§7.60):

> as long as there are prices determined by independent operators following the principle of supply and demand, even if supply or demand are affected by the government's presence in the market, there is a "market" in the sense of Article 14(d) [of the] *SCM Agreement.* (emphasis in the original)

---

[23]   In Mavroidis (2016), vol. 2, pp. 234 et seq., we offered a detailed discussion of the issue.

It held, consequently, that the US should have used the price for trees on the few private lands that still existed in Canada as the benchmark for the calculation of benefit.

The panel explicitly acknowledged that, as a matter of economic logic, the US argument stood on strong grounds. However, in the panel's view, its role was not to amend the content of a provision. That role had been assigned to the WTO membership. Consequently, even though the panel itself had not been persuaded by the logic prevailing in the relevant SCM provision, it felt that it was not empowered to undo the equilibrium struck by the framers of the SCM Agreement (§§7.58–60 of the report).

The Appellate Body overturned the panel's decision, stating that it could well be the case that the subsidizer's market is so distorted by the government's financial contribution, that using the prices prevailing therein as a benchmark for calculating the amount of subsidy conferred, might have been inappropriate. It could be the case, in other words, that no market conditions at all existed in Canada, and then recourse to out of country benchmarks should be allowed (§90):

> investigating authorities may use a benchmark other than private prices in the country of provision under Article 14(d), if it is first established that private prices in that country are distorted because of the government's predominant role in providing those goods.

In the Appellate Body's view, Article 14 of SCM reflected "guidelines", that is, this provision did not reflect a rigid rule that foresaw each and every foreseeable situation (§92). As a result, deviations, to the extent "reasonable", were warranted when a "new" situation (e.g., a factual situation that had not been included in the body of Article 14 of SCM) arose, to honor the spirit of this provision. Only this interpretation was, in the eyes of the Appellate Body, consistent with the objective of Article 14(d) of SCM, which is to establish whether the recipient is better off than it would have been without the government's financial contribution (§93):

> Under the approach advocated by the Panel (that is, private prices in the country of provision must be used whenever they exist), however, there may be situations in which there is no way of telling whether the recipient is "better off" absent the financial contribution. This is because the government's role in providing the financial contribution is so predominant that it effectively determines the price at which private suppliers sell the same or similar goods, so that the comparison contemplated by Article 14 would become circular.

The Appellate Body thus concluded that the Canadian market was so distorted that it could not serve as benchmark. More generally, it would not have been possible, in its view, to have used Canadian market prices to calculate the benefit when the government's participation in the market as provider of the same or similar goods was so predominant that private suppliers would align their prices to those of the government-provided goods (§§95 et seq., and especially 101). The Appellate Body added, nevertheless, a caveat to the effect that determination of whether private prices were distorted because of the government's predominant role in the market as a provider of certain goods, must be made on a case-by-case basis, according to the particular facts underlying each CVD investigation (§102).

There is first the legal logic of the argument advanced by the Appellate Body that we need to tackle. Let us agree, for a moment, with the Appellate Body, that the term "guideline" allows for discretion. And let us follow its reasoning one step further and look for information that would allow the judge to detect the "spirit" of the provision. Where should the Appellate Body have looked for information to this effect? The obvious place to start would be the negotiating record. The Appellate Body did not check it at all. It saw a legislative shortcoming, and corrected it through judicial activism. The premise though of the SCM Agreement is that market conditions exist in a given market, and a specific government intervention alters the conditions of competition for some producers. It is not that markets are so heavily distorted anyway that no reliable market price can be used as a benchmark to derive the amount of benefit bestowed. It is against this background that the SCM Agreement was negotiated, to a large extent, between two market economies, the EU and the US. And if it is indeed the case, that this premise is at odds with the reality in some markets, then, it is not for courts to re-write the agreement.

True, Article 14 of SCM uses the term "guidelines", but it requests that WTO members observe "the following" guidelines, not just any guidelines. The introductory paragraph of Article 14 of SCM, from which the Appellate Body selectively quoted, reads: "Furthermore, any such method shall be consistent with *the* following guidelines" (emphasis added).

The guidelines enlisted in the body of Article 14 od SCM share one feature: they all use "in country" benchmarks, that is, the prevailing market conditions in the subsidizing WTO member as a pre-condition for calculating the benefit bestowed through subsequent government action. Panels and the Appellate Body can of course, use discretion, but within the realm of the guidelines, and not beyond that realm. The US was using an "out of country" benchmark, that is the prevailing prices in countries other than Canada.

But there is also a more aggregate question of what the legal logic should be. If the overarching purpose is to find a reasonable benchmark to compare actual behavior and establish the magnitude of benefit conferred, is the list embedded in Article 14 of the SCM Agreement fit for purpose? If not, whose reasonableness matters? The principals' or the agents'? The panel's approach (spotting the problem and signaling it to law-makers) offers undeniable benefits from an institutional perspective. The Appellate Body flirted and succumbed to judicial activism in this case.

Siding with the succinct analysis of Bingham (2011)[24] and others, the rationale for sanctioning judicial activism has to do with the resulting uncertainty as to what exactly has been contracted. If WTO adjudicators were to disregard the contract, they would not be simply violating Article 3.2 of DSU. They would render it uncertain, and maybe obsolete.

1.2.4.   *Non liquet* in the WTO?

Non liquet is Latin for "it is not clear". *Non liquet* refers to a situation where the legal regime is incomplete, or unclear, and the question becomes whether it is for the judge to "complete" or "clarify" an issue. It is a contentious issue in the doctrine. No lesser lawyers than Charles Rousseau and Sir Gerald Fitzmaurice have argued, with variations between them, in favor of the existence of *non liquet*, whereas Sir Hersch Lauterpacht has defended the opposite.[25] The heart of the disagreement is this: *non liquet* should not be equated to cases where a court can (or cannot) issue a decision because courts, as we explain in what follows, always do decide. The question rather should be whether courts must issue a decision, even when they lack the means to do so. It is an issue that has pre-occupied lawmakers since time immemorial. Fuller (1969) mentions that the Code of Justinian addressed this issue head on:

> ... if anything shall seem doubtful, let it be referred by the judges to the Imperial Throne and it shall be made plain by Imperial authority, to which alone is given the right both to establish and to interpret laws. (p. 30)

International courts always strive to respond to questions, and the International Law Commission (ILC) in its Draft Convention on the Arbitral Procedure (1953) went so far as to state: "The tribunal may not bring in a finding of non liquet on the ground of the silence or Obscurity of international law or the compromise".[26]

---

[24]   Tom Bingham. 2011. The Rule of Law, Penguin Books: London, United Kingdom, at pp. 45 et seq.

[25]   Gerald Fitzmaurice. 1974. The Problem of *Non Liquet*: Prolegomena to a Restatement, pp. 89–112 in Mélanges offerts a Charles Rousseau: La Communauté Internationale, Pédone: Paris, France; Julius Stone. 1954. Lega Controls of International Conflict, Stevens and Sons: London, United Kingdom.

[26]   Quoted in Lauterpacht (1958) at p. 196, see Hersch Lauterpacht. 1958. Some Observations on the Prohibition of 'Non Liquet' and the Completeness of the Law, pp. 196–221 in Frederik M. van Asbeck (ed.). Symbolae Verzijl: Présentées au Prof

This issue made headlines when the ICJ, in its decision on the Legality of the Threat or Use of Nuclear Weapons (an Advisory Opinion),[27] held in §105: "the Court could not conclude definitively whether the threat or use of nuclear weapons would be lawful or unlawful".

This was an advisory opinion, and an explicit finding of *non liquet*. It raised the question whether *non liquet* was after all a possibility in international law. Some held that, if at all, this could be the case only when a court is called to issue an advisory opinion, whereas the majority has refuted the possibility altogether. Interestingly, even those opposing *non liquet*, do not deny that (international) law is "incomplete". Lauterpacht (1958) for example, has stated that the prohibition could be interpreted as implicit acceptance of gaps in international law,[28] and the question for the judge is to understand its duty as akin to completing the gap.

Weil (1998)[29] mentions the two claims advanced to argue that there is no room for *non liquet* in international law:

- First, the international law system has built-in safeguards (general principles of law and equity);[30] and/or
- Second, the system is logically complete, in the sense that anything that is not prohibited by public international law, is permitted for international actors. This is the notorious Lotus[31] judgment of the PCIJ (Permanent Court of International Justice).

Weil (1998), siding with Lauterpacht (1958), has suggested that the reason why *non liquet* has not happened in contentious proceedings (as opposed to the Nuclear Weapons case, which was an advisory opinion that the ICJ issued) is simply because of the common belief that litigation must be brought to an end (*ut sit finis litium*), irrespective whether law is "complete" or not: when parties submit voluntarily to a judge, they do so, in order to settle their dispute. *Non liquet* frustrates the will of the parties to end their dispute, and this is why academics have argued against it (and courts have discarded its existence).

Weil (1998) continues to state that both reasons mentioned to support the refutation of *non liquet*, constitute in fact proof that international law is riddled

---

J.H.W. Verzijl, à l'occasion de son LXXième anniversaire, Martinus Nijhoff: the Hague, the Netherlands.

[27]   1996 ICJ 35.

[28]   Reisman (1969) as well, has identified cases of implicit *non liquet*.

[29]   Prosper Weil. 1998. The Court Cannot Conclude Definitively, Non Liquet Revisited, Columbia Journal of Transnational Law, 36: 109–19.

[30]   But of course, taken to its extreme, this proposition amounts to asking whether one should be writing contracts at all.

[31]   SS Lotus 1927 PCIJ (Ser. A) no. 10 at 18–19.

with gaps: why would recourse to general principles be necessary if there were
no gaps in the first place? And if all that is not prohibited were permitted, how
manage the potential conflicts resulting from exercise of unbridled national
sovereignty? Recourse to general principles as autonomous source of law,
will always lead to the demise of *non liquet*, especially since, as Lauterpacht
(1958) notes, the completeness of law is a general principle in and of itself.
It thus becomes some sort of self-fulfilling prophecy: if (international) law is
complete, how could there ever be an instance of *non liquet*?[32]

Contract completeness has occupied the minds not only of international
lawyers, but of contract theorists and international economists as well. In
his contribution, Antràs (2014),[33] building on the seminal contribution by
Grossman and Hart (1986)[34] has adequately explained why in practice, trade
contracts like the WTO cannot specify what is to be done in every possible
future contingency. In fact, there is no disagreement across disciplines here.
Lauterpacht, a proponent of the no *non liquet* thesis, does not deny that international law is "incomplete". He simply adds that courts must rule anyway,
that is, irrespective of contractual incompleteness. Horn, Maggi and Staiger
(2010) have added an interesting dimension, namely that incompleteness is
also due to the fact that negotiators face diminishing returns. This is the case
because not all instruments (policies) affect trade in the same manner, and it
is only reasonable that negotiators focus on those that affect trade the most.
When shifting to instruments that exert less impact on trade, the outcome is not
the same, even though the effort to negotiate could be the same. Recourse to
aggregate language (vagueness) is a way to mitigate these problems (lumping
all behind the border instruments under one heading, for example). But this is
the best one can hope for and, of course, there is an associated cost inherent in
this approach: an agent (usually, a judge) asked to pronounce on an eventual
dispute, will have to dis-aggregate the language, while enjoying substantial
discretion when doing so. The risk for error increases, as it is sometimes
unclear what policies come under a heading expressed in aggregate language.
To provide but an illustration: one can easily show why freedom of establishment of foreign investors can affect sale of their traded goods. Does this mean
that WTO members must observe MFN when entering into BITs (bilateral
investment treaties)? The conventional wisdom suggests a response in the neg-

---

[32] Compare Higgins (1994).
[33] Antràs Pol. 2014. Grossman-Hart (1986) Goes Global: Incomplete Contracts,
Property Rights, and the International Organization of Production, Journal of Law,
Economics, and Organization, 30: 118–75.
[34] Sanford J. Grossman and Oliver D. Hart. 1986. The Costs and Benefits of
Ownership: A Theory of Vertical and Lateral Integration, Journal of Political Economy,
94: 691–719.

ative. But it is not the text of Article III.4 of GATT that makes this point clear. It is state practice. The contract per se is hardly clear on this score.

Since WTO contract is incomplete, should the WTO "judge" (panels and the Appellate Body) complete it, when necessary? This brings us straight into the discussion of institutional balance in the WTO that we entertained in the previous Section when discussing the reports on India—Quantitative Restrictions. While the WTO contract does assign the power to amend and interpret the covered agreements to the membership, it does not address the interplay between the legislative- and the judicial function, other than the categoric embedded in Article 3.2 of the DSU. This provision addresses of course, cases where law has been settled. But what about cases where there is observed impossibility to settle because of disagreements among parties? A notorious illustration is the outcome of the Working Party on Border Tax Adjustments, which we discuss in what follows. Before doing that though, we should briefly provide the context to this discussion.

There is not one single instance where WTO panels have pronounced a *non liquet*. And yet, there are three reasons why the claim for *non liquet* in WTO seems well-founded:

- It is WTO members that are entrusted with the exclusive competence to adopt authentic interpretations of the Agreement Establishing the WTO (Article IX.2);
- WTO panels cannot undo the balance of rights and obligations as struck by the principals (WTO members), that is, they cannot add to the obligations assumed, or diminish the rights conferred (Article 3.2 of DSU); and, finally,
- WTO practice reveals that recourse to general principles of law is not an independent source of law, but a mitigating factor which could usefully point to the correct interpretation of the WTO sources of law, that is the Agreement Establishing the WTO and its various Annexes. WTO panels have never adjudicated disputes using "equity" as the legal benchmark for pronouncing on alleged inconsistencies.

Furthermore, there is a precedent of *non liquet* in GATT/WTO jurisprudence. In 1952, the GATT panel on Belgian Family Allowances[35] faced a challenge against a Belgian measure that imposed a tax only on imports of goods originating in countries which had not implemented a system of family allowances comparable to the system that Belgium itself had implemented. This dispute placed black on white the issue how much of its behind-the-border regime a GATT member can apply to imports.

---

[35]   GATT Doc. G/32 BISD 1S/59, report of November 7, 1952.

The panel report reads like a *non liquet*. Only the words *"non liquet"* are missing from the first sentence:

> 8. The Panel felt that the legal issues involved in the complaint under consideration are such that *it would be difficult for the CONTRACTING PARTIES to arrive at a very definite ruling*. On the other hand, it was of the opinion that the Belgian legislation on family allowances was not only inconsistent with the provisions of Article I (and possibly with those of Article III, paragraph 2), but was based on a concept which was difficult to reconcile with the spirit of the General Agreement and that the CONTRACTING PARTIES should note with satisfaction the statements made at the Sixth and Seventh Sessions by the Belgian representatives and should recommend to the Belgian Government to expedite the consideration and the adoption of the necessary measures, consistent with the General Agreement, including a possible amendment of the Belgian legislation, to remove the discrimination complained of, and to refer to the CONTRACTING PARTIES not later than the first day of the Eighth Session. (emphasis added)

The panel thus refrained from providing a definitive ruling. It observed the inconsistency of the challenged measure with the spirit of the GATT, its likely inconsistency with Article III.2 of GATT (which constituted the heart of the complaint against Belgium), and left it at that. This is classic *non liquet*.

Around the same time, in the report of the Working Party on Subsidies,[36] GATT members confirmed their adherence to the origin principle with respect to direct taxes, and of the destination principle with respect to indirect taxes. This solution did not please all GATT members alike. Eventually they re-convened in a new forum to discuss this issue. The Working Party on Border Tax Adjustments,[37] produced the following outcome: there was agreement that taxes imposed directly on goods were eligible for adjustment, and further agreement that payroll (and similar) taxes, were not. The report also evidences the disagreement between members concerning the treatment of *"taxes occultes"* (e.g., taxes on capital equipment; auxiliary equipment, etc.). The GATT members included explicit reference to the disagreement in their final report, stating that, whether similar taxes could be adjusted remained an open issue.

No dispute regarding adjustment of a *"taxe occulte"* has ever been submitted to a GATT/WTO panel. Had it been the case, what should the outcome be? Should the panel go ahead and decide on an issue where the membership, convening in a non-contentious context, did not manage to agree where the law stand? Or should it simply pronounce a *non liquet*, and give the membership some additional time to ponder and "complete" the contract in this respect?

---

[36]   GATT Doc. L/1381, BISD 9S/185, report of November 19, 1960.
[37]   GATT Doc. L/3463, BISD 18S/97, report of December 2, 1970.

We submit that the latter is the wise strategy. Going gung-ho here is akin to prejudging an issue where, for example, there is a genuine disagreement between the principals. Recall, the Working Party on Border Tax Adjustments was not a panel adjudicating a dispute. There was no complainant and respondent involved. This Working Party was in a Lotus-scenario, where the PCIJ was requested to provide an advisory opinion. It was a genuine effort of the GATT membership to clarify aggregate terms like "affecting" appearing in Article III of GATT. It did not arrive at this common understanding. When principals fail to settle the law, it is not for agents to do so. For if they did, they would be trespassing their mandate as clearly established in Article 3.2 of the DSU. Furthermore, the cost of error should also guide the manner in which judicial discretion is exercised. There are some "easy" cases to adjudicate, where disputes might yet (and do, in practice) arise for opportunistic reasons. For example, every time the law-maker has included an indicative list of allowed or prohibited practices, and a dispute concerns one of the practices mentioned in the list, then the outcome is quite clear. In the presence of a clear legislative mandate (even if expressed in aggregate manner), the judge also feels secure to decide an issue (at a dis-aggregated level). When law is missing, this security is missing. And in between these extremes, there are numerous instances where the judge might feel more, or less, secure. How it will exercise its discretion, we submit – siding with Hoverkamp (2022) – should also be guided by an anticipation of the cost of error.[38]

To conclude, we do not observe instances of *non liquet* because of what Fitzmaurice (1974) named "formalistic devices to avoid *non liquet*" (p. 110) which courts have used, and because of judicial activism. Judicial activism

---

[38] The plea against judicial activism has been eloquently expressed in Sunstein (1999), and more recently by Justice Gorsuch during the oral arguments in *Ohio v. American Express*. Citing Easterbrook (1984), who famously cautioned against false positives, Gorsuch asks his colleagues: "why shouldn't we take Judge Easterbrook's admonition seriously, that judicial errors are a lot harder to correct than an occasional monopoly where you can hope and assume that the market will eventually correct it? Judicial errors are very difficult to correct", quoted in Hovenkamp (2022) at p. 5. See Frank H. Easterbrook. 1984. The Limits of Antitrust, Texas Law Review, 63: 1–40; Herbert Hovenkamp. 2022. Antitrust Error Costs, available at https://scholarship.law .upenn.edu/faculty_scholarship/2742/. One cannot exclude that two opposing views, for example, are in *equipoise* when law is missing or is unclear. Is, for example, the absence of cartels among the restrictive business practices sanctioned in the Telecoms Reference Paper (TRP), a voluntary limitation of its scope? Or an involuntary omission, as the panel in Mexico—Telecoms held (and went on to subject cartels under the disciplines of the TRP)? And was not the Working Party on Belgian Family Allowances wiser when it left the question submitted undecided? The membership convened later and contributed some clarifications to the scope of Article III of GATT in the realm of the Working Party on Border Tax Adjustments.

has often been, but not always, tolerated in the WTO. And we have mentioned a few instances where the good arguments lie with observing judicial errors. There is absolutely nothing wrong with WTO adjudicators considering whether they *must*, rather than whether they *can*, decide an issue. This way they will observe the institutional balance embedded in the DSU, and sensitize the membership to its (legislative) responsibilities. We hope that it is clear that we are not recommending recourse to *non liquet* ad nauseam, but instances like the Working Party on Border Tax Adjustments should serve as a warning sign to avoid deciding an issue.

Pronouncing a *non liquet* when warranted offers, in principle at least, two advantages at least:

• The institutional equilibrium of the WTO eco-system (the balance of rights and obligations) is observed; and
• From a policy perspective, the membership, armed with the information that an issue that has been debated before a panel has not been (adequately) regulated, will reflect on the need to intervene through legislative means and address the observed gap.

A pronouncement of *non liquet* is anyway consonant with Article 3.2 of DSU, and hence warranted from a legitimacy perspective. It is also warranted from an effectiveness perspective, if the *amicus* saga serves as illustration. Through their patchwork solution in US—Shrimp, the Appellate Body judges deprived the membership of the opportunity to reflect on the necessity to step in, and "complete" the contract, by adding, for example, a paragraph in Article 13 of the DSU that would explain under what conditions *amici* could file before WTO panels (and the Appellate Body). Had the Appellate Body done just that, maybe the story of filing *amicus* to the WTO would have been a happier story. As things stand, there is absolutely no basis to think that *amici* briefs have exerted any influence in the shaping of WTO case law.

In a similar vein, one might wonder whether the judicial crisis could have been averted if the Appellate Body for example, had adopted a different attitude in the context of its case law dealing with Article 17.6 of the Antidumping Agreement. This provision, which was clearly introduced at the behest of the US during the Uruguay Round, calls for panels to adopt a deferential attitude towards interpretations of law by national antidumping authorities when the latter rest on a "permissible interpretation" of the relevant law.

Panels are requested, by virtue of Article 3.2 of the DSU, to interpret WTO law in accordance with principles of customary international law. Article 11 of DSU establishes the generic standard of review for panels:

> ... a panel should make an *objective assessment* of the matter before it, including an
> objective assessment of the facts of the case and the applicability of and conformity

with the relevant covered agreements, and make such other findings as will assist the DSB in making the recommendations or in giving the rulings provided for in the covered agreements. (emphasis added)

Article 17.6 includes two distinct provisions: (i) requests from panels to establish that investigating authorities have performed an "unbiased and objective" establishment and evaluation of facts before them, whereas by virtue of (ii) panels cannot deviate from the obligation to have recourse to customary rules of interpretation. Unlike Article 11 of DSU it thus does not request an "objective assessment". In lieu of this term, Article 17.6(i) requests from panels to simply assess whether the investigating authorities complied with their obligations. Consistent case law suggests that this linguistic difference is inconsequential: panels and the Appellate Body have equated "assessment" to "objective assessment".[39]

Article 17.6(ii) requests from panels to defer to the interpretation by investigating authorities of WTO members, if they find it "permissible". *Prima facie*, this standard of review is more deferential than the combination of Articles 11 and 3.2 of DSU (which require from panels to make an objective assessment of the matter before them using the VCLT as means of interpretation). Clearly, there is a disjuncture, for if they were identical, what would have been the point of introducing both in the first place?

The working hypothesis in Article 17.6(ii) is that recourse to the VCLT does not necessarily always lead to one interpretation. Recall, Article 17.6 (ii) reads as follows:

The panel shall interpret the relevant provisions of the Agreement in accordance with customary rules of interpretation of public international law. Where the panel finds that a relevant provision of the Agreement admits of more than one *permissible* interpretation, the panel shall find the authorities' measure to be in *conformity* with the Agreement if it rests upon one of those *permissible* interpretations (emphasis added)

The Appellate Body case law on this score can be summed up in two sentences:

- An interpretation must be permissible under the VCLT (recourse to VCLT that is, should lead to a conclusion that a range of permissible interpretations was the common intent of the parties);

---

[39]   See §§72 et seq. in the WTO Analytical Index, which is available at (www.wto .org/english/res_e/publications_e/ai17_e/anti_dumping_art17_jur.pdf), where all relevant case law on this score is displayed.

and

- There is not one single instance where the Appellate Body has found that more than one interpretations were "permissible".

In fact, it is a panel (the panel on Argentina—Poultry Anti-dumping Duties) that offered the only illustration so far of "permissible" interpretation in WTO case law so far. This panel was requested to judge whether 46 percent of all domestic producers should be considered as a major proportion of the total domestic production (as per Article 4.1 of the Agreement on Antidumping). Without delving too much into a thorough discussion of this issue, the panel accepted that this was indeed a permissible interpretation of the term (§7.341). The Appellate Body never emulated an approach along these lines.

The Appellate Body might have taken the view that the VCLT always leads to one interpretation. If so, it should have stated in all its voluminous case law on this score, why this has been the case.[40] Actually, the back and forth in its case law in some instances (like the interpretation of "less favorable treatment", "pass through", etc.) provides ample evidence that the Appellate Body does not believe that only one interpretation is possible whenever recourse to the VCLT has been made. But even if it did hold this view, it should have referred the issue back to the membership, since, in this case, it would be effectively holding that Article 17.6(ii) does not make sense. Recall, by virtue of the VCLT, the Appellate Body cannot interpret any term to redundancy ("effective treaty interpretation"). If recourse to VCLT always leads to one interpretation, what was the point of adding the reference to "permissible" interpretations in the body of Article 17.6(ii) in the first place?

If, on the other hand, the Appellate Body had thought (and quite legitimately so) that the consequences of introducing Article 17.6 were unclear, well, it should have equally well sent the ball back to the membership, requesting from it to clarify this provision. There is an instrument designed specifically for similar occasions: Article IX.2 of the Agreement establishing the WTO entrusts the Ministerial Conference (General Council) with the right to adopt interpretations of the terms appearing already in the various WTO agreements. The Appellate Body did not avail itself of the possibility to send the question back to the membership recommending that it adopted an interpretation under Article IX.2. The rest is history, and so it seems, is the Appellate Body.

---

[40]   The leading cases are US—Hot Rolled Steel, §§59 et seq., and US—Continued Zeroing, §§267 et seq.

1.3. Have WTO Courts Respected their Agency Contract?

We have provided a few examples already of procedural innovations. Alas, the frontier between non-functional and dysfunctional proved to be a line in the sand. No WTO member ever complained about the fact that WTO courts took it upon them to decide on allocation of burden of proof. But a special session was convened to discuss the Appellate Body initiative with respect to *amicus* briefs, evidencing a collective displeasure against the Appellate Body's initiative to accept *amicus* briefs. And in between these two extremes, lie initiatives like bestowing enhanced third party rights, and completing the analysis. Even though no similar procedural rights had been agreed by the DSU framers, it seems safe to conclude that WTO members have acquiesced: they do not complain whenever the Appellate Body completes the analysis, and they routinely request enhanced third-party rights.

All this is to say that there have been a few cases already where doubts can legitimately be raised when asking whether WTO members have observed their mandate. But the overwhelming majority of "innovative" initiatives that the Appellate Body has introduced, have been met with the acquiescence of the vast majority of the membership. Agency costs were judged intolerable only by the US, and the US reaction sufficed for what happened recently: we ended up in the provisional demise of the dispute regime of the WTO.

In a recent document, the Congressional Research Service (CRS), an agency that works exclusively for the United States Congress providing policy and legal analysis to committees and Members of both the House and Senate regardless of party affiliation, has put together all of the critique that successive US administrations have voiced against the WTO Appellate Body.[41] This publication divides WTO reports into two categories, namely, poor outcomes, and reports where the Appellate Body has trespassed its mandate. While there is little overlap between the cases we have mentioned and the cases featured in this report, the fact of the matter remains that WTO courts have not always acted as agents.

---

[41] Nina M. Hart, and Brandon J. Murrill. 2021. The World Trade Organization's (WTO's) Appellate Body: Key Disputes and Controversies, Congressional Research Service, R46852: Washington D.C.

8. Noisy judgments, legal uncertainty, and beyond: cut the coat according to the cloth

1. CONCLUDING DISCUSSION

In this concluding chapter, we would like to briefly recap the main conclusions of our study, before adding a few words about the institutional dimension of our discussion.

1.1. The Key Takeaways

The statutory language of the DSU should leave no doubt that the legislative intent was that only the covered agreements should enjoy the status of "sources of WTO law". The covered agreements provide the various WTO bodies with the requisite powers to add to the WTO "primary" law, by adopting interpretations, amendments, decisions, what we referred to as "secondary" law. And this is where the buck stops, when it comes to detailing the various WTO sources of law.

As feasible agreements are "incomplete", for good reasons as well, disputes regarding their understanding might arise. The WTO, in contrast to the overwhelming majority of international integration processes, includes a compulsory third-party adjudication regime, the DSU. WTO judges (panelists and Appellate Body members) are exclusively competent to resolve disputes. They must do that without undoing the balance of rights and obligations agreed by the membership. And they must also do that by using the customary rules of interpretation of international agreements, the VCLT. The VCLT is not a substitute for legal methodology, but it provides the means to identify interpretative elements, and classify them under its headings.

WTO adjudicators have to a great extent respected the agency contract embedded in Article 3.2 of the DSU, but we observed some occasional deviations where the Appellate Body especially has misconstrued obligations both of procedural as well as of substantive nature. But this is hardly the direct outcome of the manner in which they have used the VCLT.

Against this background, what are the key takeaways of our empirical analysis in Chapters 5 and 7? There are two. First, the WTO adjudicators have largely used the VCLT in perfunctory manner, *pro forma*. Second, not only have WTO adjudicators "liberated" themselves from the VCLT, but they also understood their mandate as a "license to adjudicate". We explain.

The covered agreements are "incomplete" in terms of regulating the procedures, and invite discretion with respect to the elements that could be used to interpret the substantive provisions. Through their actions, WTO adjudicators have added some procedural innovations, the overwhelming majority of which were met with the members' acquiescence. In that, the agency costs have been tolerable (for all but one member).

They have also erroneously classified some sources under VCLT headings. And they have overlooked useful sources of information as well. They have thus committed errors both with respect to the extensive as well as the intensive margin of interpretative elements of VCLT, and have further committed both false positives, as well as false negatives.

We should note, in their defense, a redeeming factor (besides contract incompleteness, that is). WTO adjudicators have been, for all practical purposes, operating in a context of legislative inertia. The WTO legislative activity has been modest at best, and eventually this takes its toll, as the only bridge to modernity is through the WTO judiciary. WTO courts might have felt the pressure to act on occasion as substitute for the missing legislative guidance. The DSU Review could have provided some solutions, but did not. Even in areas where practice had solved problems that appeared in the past (like the sequencing issue),[1] the DSU Review did not manage to crystallize the existing consensus into statutory language.

---

[1]   In the early WTO years, the issue of "sequencing" (should request to retaliate always follow the process before a compliance panel/Appellate Body?) raised a few eyebrows, and provoked some discussions. The reason was that the wording of Article 22.2 of the DSU provided for a 20-day period from the end of the RPT, during which a request to authorize retaliation would have to be submitted. So, what if the establishment of a compliance panel had been requested, since there was disagreement between the disputing parties as to whether compliance had been achieved? In this case, the 20-day deadline would have lapsed. Would then a request to establish a compliance panel effectively reduce the right to request authorization to retaliate to redundancy? WTO members though, observed sequencing in practice. The long list of agreements to observe sequencing is the best testimony to this effect (www.wto.org/english/res_e/publications_e/ai17_e/dsu_art21_oth.pdf at p. 5). During the DSU Review, there was a large consensus behind the crystallization of practice into law, as McDougall (2018) reports. Nothing concrete happened, precisely because nothing in general happened in the realm of the DSU Review.

There are counter-arguments, of course. WTO adjudicators are not, by statutory fiat, legislators (Article 3.2 of the DSU). Under the circumstances, one might have legitimately expected that absence of legislative guidance would have reinforced and intensified the argument for recourse to *non liquet*. Not that similar arguments had not been present since the advent of the WTO. Even though the Uruguay Round was concluded during the apex of liberalism following the fall of the Berlin Wall, it did reflect a few uneasy compromises, especially in the realm of contingent protection instruments. It is not only the controversy with Article 17.6 of the Agreement on Antidumping. Our discussion of the jurisprudence under Article 14 of SCM as well fits this bill to perfection, and probably a clarification of the content-differentiation between customary rules of interpretation and "permissible interpretations" should have been sought as well.

When deciding under uncertainty, the cost of error matters. Even if the probability to err is the same, the stakes could be asymmetric. Erring on the side of caution (conservative judgment) might at most make one disputing party unhappy, for it did not secure a judgment in its favor. But it has not lost the argument either. Erring, conversely, when adopting a gung-ho attitude (prejudging the status of law, when the judge has very little information to go by in the first place), will not only make one side unhappy (for losing an argument that it should not have lost). It will impose costs on the rest of the membership, as the case law developed will have to be reproduced in future litigation as well. It is not accidental that panels and the Appellate Body adopted a very conservative attitude towards *amicus curiae* briefs, practically reducing them to irrelevance following the first judgment in US-Shrimp.

And to cap it all off, WTO adjudicators have classified almost all valuable sources that could help them reason better their decision under supplementary means. The unavoidable consequence is that recourse will be made sparingly, and as we have shown, in the overwhelming majority of cases in order to confirm an existing interpretation, and not in order to illuminate and enrich the interpretative process. The VCLT ended up being used routinely as supplementary means to an esoteric process that panels and the Appellate Body have developed over the years: it has often served as confirmation for opinions reached in spite of the interpretative elements included in the VCLT. We can legitimately take issue with the treatment of the Modalities paper, a document that served as basis for the entire membership to commit to during the negotiation, as the reasons why it is not considered historical context are unpersuasive. We will not know why the "Oilseeds agreement" is not historical context either. Case law does not reflect any discussion of the negotiation of Article 14 of the SCM, which led the Appellate Body to overlook the letter of this provision in interpreting it *contra legem*. Case law reflects only a superficial discussion of the negotiation of Article 10 of the Agreement on Agriculture (majority opinion), and/or of Article 17.6 of the Agreement on Antidumping. This is not satisfactory.

1.2.   The New OK (Is it OK, or Have We Lost Our Way?)

In its first ever report, the WTO Appellate Body stated that the Agreement Establishing the WTO (and its annexes, that is all covered agreements) "is not to be read in clinical isolation from public international law".[2]

Why was this statement necessary? After all, the DSU as we saw did build a bridge to public international law, when acknowledging the relevance of customary rules of interpretation in its Article 3.2, did it not? Probably, the Appellate Body wanted to underscore that a page was being turned with the passage from the GATT to the WTO. For the GATT years were quite different in this respect. Academics and researchers that have looked in detail into GATT practice in the realm of adjudication, have unanimously concluded that the GATT, in this respect, was akin to a self-contained regime.[3] This term denotes regimes that shield themselves away from influence of public international law (and especially the law on state responsibility).[4]

The majority of the cited studies concern the earlier years of the GATT. The situation started to change as of the 1980s with the establishment of the Legal Office, and the (gradual) professionalization of legal advice supplied to panels by individuals trained in international law (as well).[5] References to international law continued to be scarce.

Take, for example, the GATT panel report on US—Tuna I (Mexico) issued on September 3, 1991, in the last years of the GATT. This report dealt with the

---

[2]   US—Gasoline at p. 17. The Appellate Body elaborated on this statement in its report on US—Shrimp in §§154 et seq.
[3]   Willem Riphagen. 1982. Third Report on State Responsibility, International Law Commission (ILC) Yearbook, Vol. II, Part One, United Nations: New York City, New York; Gaetano Arangio-Ruiz. 1992. Fourth Report on State Responsibility, ILC Year-book, Vol. II, Part One, United Nations: New York City, New York; Bruno Simma and Dirk Pulkowski. 2006. Of Planets and the Universe: Self-contained Regimes in International Law, European Journal of International Law, 17: 483–529; Pieter Jan Kuijper. 1994. The Law of GATT as a Special Field of International Law: Ignorance, Further refinement or Self-Contained System of International Law? Netherlands Yearbook of International Law, 25: 227–57; Petros C. Mavroidis. 1991. Das GATT als Self-Contained Régime, Recht der Internationalen Wirtschaft, 6: 497–501; and Benedek, op. cit.
[4]   For an authoritative analysis of the term, see Bruno Simma. 1985. Self-Contained Regimes, Netherlands Yearbook of International Law, 16: 111–36.
[5]   Various contributions in the excellent volume edited by Gabrielle Marceau underscore this point, see Gabrielle Marceau (ed.). 2015. A History of Law and Lawyers in the GATT/WTO, Cambridge University Press & the WTO: Geneva, Switzerland.

intersection of trade liberalization and (international) environmental law, and still contains no reference to multilateral environmental treaties, even though both the respondent, as well as various third parties had explicitly referred to numerous similar treaties.[6] The same report evidences no mention of the VCLT, either.

But a few other reports issued during the GATT's last years did explicitly mention the VCLT, and interpreted the GATT through recourse to its disciplines.[7] Viewed in its historical context, Article 3.2 of DSU audaciously crystallized into law the prevailing, later GATT practice, even though there was no unanimity in GATT practice as to its relevance.

Thus, the above quoted Appellate Body statement effectively amounts to an acknowledgment that the door to international law had been opened, but through its threshold, only the VCLT could step into the WTO legal order. WTO members could be condemned for violating Articles III/XX of GATT, but not for violating the CITES convention (Convention on International Trade in Endangered Species) convention. CITES, at most, could be used to interpret the relevant GATT provisions. This much is of course, the correct approach. But as already argued, it is the WTO adjudicators' haphazard understanding of the VCLT, that has created problems.

The VCLT is a very intuitive treaty, and this is probably the reason why it has been elevated to customary international law. Think of the VCLT in the hands of a GATT practitioner with no training at all in public international law. He/she, when called to interpret a provision, would look into the words in light of the negotiation where he/she participated and the questions asked at that stage. Subsequent practice/agreement that corrected some initial lack of clarity, or adjusted the GATT to new needs, is, as well, the bread and butter of the practitioner. All those elements are of course, part and parcel of the VCLT system.

But the rest matters as well. Consider, for example, features of policy coherence (other relevant rules of international law, etc.).[8] This is the domain

---

[6]   The full report is reproduced in the official WTO webpage at www.wto.org/english/tratop_e/dispu_e/gatt_e/91tuna.pdf.

[7]   We discussed all this in Mavroidis (2022) op. cit., Chapter 2.

[8]   There is, of course, no aggregate obligation mandating that governments behave in the realm of international relations in coherent manner. In fact, they often maximize welfare by being incoherent. International lawyers especially, and policy analysts to a lesser extent, have underlined the problems posed by what has been termed "fragmentation" of international law. Of course, this term is abusive, as international law exists to the extent there are gains from cooperation. And nations had no trouble in contracting obligations to behave in consistent manner when warranted, as in Article 5.5 of WTO Agreement on Sanitary and Phyto-sanitary Measures. Usually, as in the aforementioned case, the requirement for consistency is at disaggregated, well-specified

of those entrusted with policy planning, as well as public international lawyers. The GATT practitioner will not necessarily be informed about these developments, of which his/her government is of course aware.

The point is this. In the hands of individuals with different skills, the value of the same interpretative element might be increased or decreased. This is a risk especially in WTO practice, where recourse to supplementary means of interpretation is, on occasion, haphazard, as we have seen. But there is an additional issue, and this is the key point in this section. There are few renaissance men and women, so network externalities across members of a judicial body are the best guarantee to do justice to the very demanding test put together by the VCLT. The original Appellate Body, the rule-setter in the first 25 years of the WTO regarding disputed issues of law, was composed of individuals with different skills. There was some overlap between them, but there was a lot of complementarity as well: three renowned international lawyers (Fiorentino Feliciano, Mitsuo Matsushita and Chris Beeby), Europe's most experienced EU lawyer (Claus-Dieter Ehlermann), a trained economist (Said El Naggar), a lawyer with astute political judgment (Jim Bacchus), and to top it all off, GATT's oldest hand, Julio Lacarte-Murò, who had participated in the original GATT negotiation, had worked for the GATT, was his country's (Uruguay) delegate to the GATT, lived through all GATT rounds, and eventually was nominated at the bench. With this mix of talents, there was legitimate expectation that no stone would be left unturned, and attention would be paid to all VCLT elements.

And they could rely on advice by Debra Steger, the Canadian delegate in the DSU negotiation, who had in the meantime become the Head of the Legal Service of the Appellate Body, and Bill Davey, a pre-eminent trade scholar, who headed the WTO Legal Service. Haass (2017) has taken the view that the survival of a regime should not be contingent upon bringing in extraordinary talents to serve it:

> One factor … increasing the odds that world order will survive is that it not require talented statesmen, the supply of which is likely to be insufficient … Individuals of mediocre or poor skills will enter into positions of responsibility.[9]

---

level that judges can police without emerging as world government types. For an excellent discussion on fragmentation, and the challenges it poses, see Eyal Benvenisti and George W. Downs. 2007. The Empire's New Clothes: Political Economy and the Fragmentation of International Law, Stanford Law Review, 60: 595–631.

[9]   Richard N. Haass. 2017. A World in Disarray, Penguin Books: New York City, New York (at p. 118).

There is no guarantee that equally talented individuals will consistently occupy decisive posts, neither in the WTO nor in any other context. But a few tips could reduce unjustified inconsistencies across cases, which are perilous for the institution per se. We turn to this discussion in the next sub-section. But for now, the main takeaway of the discussion is that, although the VCLT seems to encompass all there is to reflect upon when trying to interpret an agreement like the WTO, in the hands of different people it can lead to different results.

1.3.   The Institutional Dimension (Reducing the Potential for Noisy Judgments)

Judgment, as Kahneman et al. (2021) have aptly put it, is measurement, and the instrument is the human mind (p. 39).[10] Who is appointed at the bench matters. While digitalization can help with issues like access to justice, as a recent report issued by the Council of Europe has concluded, reflecting the common-place view in this respect,[11] we are still some way before we can confidently replace human with digital justice. Judges are, in the short- to medium-term, necessary.

Recall that while the sources of WTO law are well-defined in the legislative documents, their interpretation matters, as the majority of the obligations assumed are standards, malleable in the hands of adjudicators. And, recall further that the WTO judge is in a non-enviable position as she/he will be called to deal with two incomplete contracts, the WTO itself, and its interpretative means, the VCLT. The coefficient of importance of the various elements embedded in VCLT is a judgment call. Practice shows that the classification of elements under one or the other category is equally a judgment call, and we pointed to a few false negatives, a few false positives, and also to inconsistencies in the classification of interpretative elements. Errors and incoherence are both problematic. Whereas the former is usually referred to as "biased judgment", the latter is what Kahneman et al. (2021) would call "noisy judgments", and WTO practice offers a plethora of them.

Noisy judgments are problematic, first and foremost, because they create legal uncertainty. Indeed, if the function of prior judgments is to inform the judge about how terms are understood, conflicting (noisy) judgments simply do not provide this service. They also undermine the authority of the adjudicator, who is not supposed to serve different sauce to the goose and the gander,

---

[10]   Daniel Kahneman, Olivier Sibony and Cass R. Sunstein. 2021. Noise, a Flaw in Human Judgment, Little Brown Spark: New York, Boston, London.
[11]   See   www.consilium.europa.eu/en/press/press-releases/2020/10/13/digital -justice-council-adopts-conclusions-on-digitalisation-to-improve-access-to-justice/.

and incite all sorts of suspicion across those submitting disputes. And, finally, by construction, they cannot all be right. Noisy judgments thus are inherently flawed.

To avoid any misunderstanding here on the use of the term, a judgment is noisy when the same canon is interpreted in different ways when no differentiating factors justifying the deviation exist. In presence of differentiating factors, one cannot even start speaking of noisy judgments.

The Appellate Body has bought (some) insurance policy against noisy judgments. It observes collegiality: in order to ensure consistency and coherence in case law, all Appellate Body members will meet regularly to discuss matters of policy, practice and procedure, and, of course, the resolution of issues presented in the realm of specific disputes (Rule 4 of the Appellate Body Working Procedures).[12] But it has not avoided "noise".

Mindful of the limits of point-to-point comparisons, we compare the attitude of three different Appellate Body compositions towards international law. We have picked three disputes (US—Gasoline; US—Shrimp; EC—Seal Products), of comparable subject-matter (Article XX of GATT, and more specifically, protection of environment, an area where there are gains from cooperation, and various international agreements have been signed to this effect).[13] We want to examine the attitude of successive Appellate Body compositions towards this body of law. We confine this brief discussion to the Appellate Body for an obvious reason: unlike panels, the term of Appellate Body members is not exhausted in the resolution of one dispute. And since it is the hierarchically higher body, it is also the precedent-setter, in the sense that, even though there is no *stare decisis* in the WTO legal order, the Appellate Body is the organ to provide coherence and consistency in the development of the body of law.

The first Appellate Body comprised four individuals who were fully-fledged international lawyers (Christopher Beeby, Claus-Dieter Ehlermann, Fiorentino Feliciano and Mitsuo Matsushita). In US—Gasoline, we counted eight ref-

---

[12] WTO Doc. WT/AB/WP/6 of August 16, 2010. Julio Lacarte-Muró, an old GATT hand who had participated in the negotiation of the GATT and eventually became a member of the Appellate Body, used to say that collegiality came at a price, since the Appellate Body members had to invest time and effort in order to effectively participate in discussions. Anecdotally, he recalled an episode where the three members of the Division were of one view, and the four non-members, of another. And yet, they continued to talk until they had reached a compromise. This was quite wise, since the four non-members might have been called in the future to deal with the same issue. By having them on board, the Appellate Body could avoid future embarrassments, see www.acwl.ch/interview-with-ambassador-julio-lacarte-muro/.

[13] Because of the short terms that Appellate Body members serve, it is difficult to establish trends across issues. Some members of the Appellate Body only had the chance to deal with a very narrow set of disputes.

erences to public international law (international agreements; ICJ decisions; doctrine) in pages 17, 20 and 21 and footnotes 33, 34, 45, 46 and 52.

In the second Appellate Body, some of the original members were still present, and another international lawyer joined (Yasuhei Taniguchi). In US—Shrimp, we counted 16 references to public international law, in §§130, 132, 154, 157, 167, 168, 169 and 171, and footnotes 109, 110, 111, 113, 116, 136, 170 and 177. In EC—Seal Products (the third Appellate Body), there is no public international lawyer on the bench, and we count only two references to public international law (§§5.138, 5.305).

Incoherence in WTO practice is not limited to classification of interpretative elements. Recall our discussion about key terms such as "less favorable treatment", and "pass through". There are also many more examples. The manner in which sources are interpreted has been erratic, largely because of the compartmentalized manner in which the rule of interpretation embedded in the VCLT has been used.[14] Errors have been committed, and we have pointed to a few in the preceding pages, where by no means we purported an exhaustive analysis.[15] And some might claim that we are making a mountain out of a molehill, as errors, judicial errors that is, occur in domestic setting as well without much fanfare surrounding them.

The volume of cases, and the significance of errors, are different in a domestic and a foreign setting. An error in between 10,000 cases adjudicated per year is one thing. An error in every four to five cases is another. And, alas, an error when discussing the relevance of an interpretative element of a WTO obligation is not self-contained either. It affects the end result. Errors by domestic courts are addressed more easily, through the passage of a domestic statute. Errors by international courts are more difficult to address through subsequent adjudication (and the ensuing pre-emption it will exercise on judicial discretion).

And errors by international adjudicators are costly, as they contribute to undermining the confidence in international adjudication. In a domestic-law setting, this is substantially less of an issue. Just pause for a moment, and

---

[14] WTO judges typically divide their discussions in various segments, starting from text where they conclude before moving to context, etc. A brief perusal of reports suffices to persuade the reader that this has been routinely the case. Exceptionally only, some judges will hold judgment until they have exhausted the various elements of the VCLT.

[15] Case law has been critically discussed since 2000 by a group of economists and lawyers, and published in the World Trade Review. The conclusions of different authors who have participated in the review over the years until 2019 (when the Appellate Body was dissolved) are quite similar in this respect, see e.g., www.cambridge.org/core/journals/world-trade-review/issue/E9058D3DE4F396AFCA0A9D4D45C7A1F3.

reflect. How would case law on Article XVII of the GATT have looked like, had the drafters of Canada—Wheat Exports and Grain Imports spent some time going through the voluminous negotiating record, which makes it clear that state-trading enterprises are an exception to the rule, and must behave like private agents? And then think of the spillover effects. Had they established then that price discrimination (a perfectly rational conduct for private agents) should not be confused with non-discrimination (as embedded in Article I of GATT), how would the case law on "public bodies" of Article of SCM Agreement look?

And there are so many more examples. How could the US—Tuna II (Mexico) panel and Appellate Body overlook that conformity assessment procedures are the necessary threshold question when establishing likeness (and not consumers as in Article III of GATT)? A simple perusal of the negotiating history of the negotiating record of the TBT Agreement would have made it obvious that the whole purpose of conformity assessment is to substitute equivalence/substitutability of goods as consumers understand it. The TBT covers cases where governments and consumers have different preferences (as it deals with experience and sometimes with credence goods, and not with search goods), otherwise why regulate in the first place?[16]

Attempts to "complete" ex ante will not fail by construction. Irrespective of the legal qualification of acts by the WTO organs, "completion" of the contract has been successfully tried on various occasions. There are no interpretations adopted so far as per Article IX.2 of the Agreement Establishing the WTO. But there are other ways to accomplish a similar function.

Paragraph 5.2 of the Doha Ministerial Decision, which defined the term "reasonable interval" appearing in Article 2.12 of the TBT Agreement to cover a period of at least six months, was considered by WTO adjudicating bodies a "subsequent agreement" between the members in the sense of Article 31 VCLT. The membership is now safe in the knowledge that, in the circumstances envisaged in the Ministerial Decision, it cannot be challenged for inaction for less than six months. In similar vein, the ADP Committee's initiatives aiming to interpret POI guide subsequent practice in this area.

There are good reasons why more, along these lines, can be accomplished in the future. We signaled already that recourse, when warranted, to indicative lists, will help the judge avoid false negatives (type II errors). Case law could be an important input in this vein. There is of course an institutional challenge lying ahead, in the sense of who should be entrusted with the task to put together case law of key terms where disputes arise frequently? A task

---

[16]   Petros C. Mavroidis. 2019. Last Mile for Tuna (to a Safe Harbour): What is the TBT Agreement All About? European Journal of International Law, 30: 279–301.

force comprising both members of the Secretariat, as well as a few delegates representing the membership, could provide the response to this question. Its work would then be submitted for consideration, and eventually, revive the moribund Article IX.2 of the Agreement Establishing the WTO.

A note of caution seems warranted here. Stith and Cabranes (1998)[17] discuss the US Sentencing Guidelines, which were meant to reduce inter-judge sentence variation (a much narrower focus than interpretation), and conclude that this has hardly been the case in practice (pp. 105 et seq.). They distinguish between "open" and "hidden" discretion (the former referring to explicit, statutory discretion, and the latter to the inherent judicial discretion to subject facts to a rule of law), and conclude that the latter has been proved hard to tame in US practice, the attempts for "completing" the contract notwithstanding. They consequently recommend that what matters most is to ensure that through the selection process, the fittest will be called to the bench (pp. 170 et seq.). This is our recommendation as well, especially as, once the necessary adjustments have been made, the hidden discretion is exacerbated by the compulsory recourse to the VCLT.

The institutional dimension matters as well, and it matters a lot. The current mode for selecting panelists to serve on an ad hoc basis certainly does not help. For WTO adjudicators to adopt a coherent attitude towards the VCLT, some adjustments should be made. By adding new individuals every time, the potential for deviation and differentiation increases. A system of permanent panelists, or even of chairs that serve for a time-bound mandate (as in Article 19.11.6 of the Comprehensive and Progressive Agreement for Trans-Pacific Partnership) would be a facilitating factor.

And then, those called to the bench following a rigorous process will serve the institution better if when in doubt, they respect *in dubio mitius* more. The understanding that WTO adjudicators develop towards Article 11 of DSU matters, and matters quite a lot. Recall, this provision in part reads: "… and make such other findings as will assist the DSB in making the recommendations or in giving the rulings provided for in the covered agreements".

This sentence includes an inducement, an encouragement of sorts, for WTO adjudicators not to judge beyond what is necessary to resolve a dispute, within of course the confines of the sources of law as discussed in this volume.

The sources of law though, while clearly stated in the WTO contract, can be over- or under-interpreted because of (through the) use of the VCLT. While a WTO panel cannot find against Home for violating the CITES convention, it can use CITES to understand and interpret Article XX(b) of GATT. There

---

[17] Kate Stith and José A. Cabranes. 1998. Fear of Judging, The University of Chicago Press: Chicago, Illinois.

are some fine lines here that a careless judge might easily cross. This is one reason why, when adjudicating a dispute, they should not feel obliged to decide under any circumstances. There is absolutely nothing wrong with issuing a *non liquet*, when warranted. The logic of the VCLT is the opposite of endogenous judgments. It is through the exploration of the various elements included therein that the agent will observe the agency contract while arriving at a reasonable conclusion. The quality of the judgment is enriched through the consideration of the elements reflected in Articles 31 and 32, and the eventual outcome depends on all and not some of them. This is probably the most valuable lesson of our discussion.

Whenever WTO adjudicators feel that the legal framework before them is wanting or unclear as to what exactly has been committed, they should send the ball back to the legislators' room. It is wiser to commit a false negative whenever doubts as to the scope of obligations assumed emerge, than a false positive. This is of course, what they must do anyway, if they are to respect the agency contract that binds their discretion.

Finally, Rosenne's admonition "precedents may be followed or discarded, but not disregarded", should be the guiding directive for all WTO adjudicators. This is particularly important both in terms of defining the extensive margin, as well as the intensive margin of interpretative elements used. And of course, in cases where the precedent has been discarded, adjudicators should explain why this has been the case. In the elaborate terms that Lord Denning put it (2005):

> Just as the scientist takes his instances and from them builds up his general propositions, so the lawyer should take his precedents and from them build his general principles. Just as the propositions of the scientist fall to be modified when shown not to fit all instances, or even discarded when shown to be in error, so the principles of the lawyer should be modified when found to be unsuited to the times or discarded when found to work injustice.[18]

Respect for the precedent will greatly enhance the harmonious understanding of the VCLT in adjudicatory practice at the WTO level. Respect should not be confused with compulsory, necessary adherence to whatever has been decided in a prior case. Disagreements are legitimate, and there are even gains from innovation that future practice can reap. But, while divergence from prior decisions is legitimate, prior decisions must be discussed. The adjudicator who turns a blind eye to whatever the court has decided before on the same issue, is the easiest target to accuse for opportunistic behavior. This is precisely what should be avoided.

---

[18] Denning (2005) at p. 292. Lord Denning, of course, had studied mathematics, and taught it for a year, before studying law.

Following these guidelines, it is submitted, will contribute towards reducing noisy judgments, while reserving to adjudicators the function that they were called to serve in the WTO institutional equilibrium: that of the interpreter of a law put together by the WTO membership, and not that of the law-maker. All this suggests to us at least, that in the upcoming negotiation regarding the revamping of the DSU (which at this stage, seems uncertain), the membership should pay particular attention to the qualifications of the agents.

The WTO is not going through its best days. And yes, undeniably, the current crisis has largely contributed to the rather bleak picture we have painted in this work. Of course, more complete contracts that reduce discretion also reduce errors and the ensuing dissatisfaction. But we are going through a period where no contracts are signed at all. And the VCLT will continue to be applied as it is, irrespective of the completeness of the contract to interpret. Judges, in other words, matter, and matter even more when they have little institutional help in terms of the adequacy of the contractual expression. It is high time the trading community took this issue with the seriousness that it deserves.

Annex 1: key provisions of the DSU

ARTICLE 1 COVERAGE AND APPLICATION

1. The rules and procedures of this Understanding shall apply to disputes brought pursuant to the consultation and dispute settlement provisions of the agreements listed in Appendix 1 to this Understanding (referred to in this Understanding as the "covered agreements"). The rules and procedures of this Understanding shall also apply to consultations and the settlement of disputes between Members concerning their rights and obligations under the provisions of the Agreement Establishing the World Trade Organization (referred to in this Understanding as the "WTO Agreement") and of this Understanding taken in isolation or in combination with any other covered agreement.

ARTICLE 3 ADMINISTRATION

2. The dispute settlement system of the WTO is a central element in providing security and predictability to the multilateral trading system. The Members recognize that it serves to preserve the rights and obligations of Members under the covered agreements, and to clarify the existing provisions of those agreements in accordance with customary rules of interpretation of public international law. Recommendations and rulings of the DSB cannot add to or diminish the rights and obligations provided in the covered agreements

ARTICLE 4 GENERAL PROVISIONS

3. If a request for consultations is made pursuant to a covered agreement, the Member to which the request is made shall, unless otherwise mutually agreed, reply to the request within 10 days after the date of its receipt and shall enter into consultations in good faith within a period of no more than 30 days after the date of receipt of the request, with a view to reaching a mutually satisfactory solution. If the Member does not respond within 10 days after the date of receipt of the request, or does not enter into consultations within a period of no more than 30 days, or a period otherwise mutually agreed, after the date of receipt of the request, then the Member that requested the holding of consultations may proceed directly to request the establishment of a panel.

ARTICLE 7 TERMS OF REFERENCE OF PANELS

1. Panels shall have the following terms of reference unless the parties to the dispute agree otherwise within 20 days from the establishment of the panel:
"To examine, in the light of the relevant provisions in (name of the covered agreement(s) cited by the parties to the dispute), the matter referred to the DSB by (name of party) in document ... and to make such findings as will assist the DSB in making the recommendations or in giving the rulings provided for in that/ those agreement(s)."
2. Panels shall address the relevant provisions in any covered agreement or agreements cited by the parties to the dispute.
3. In establishing a panel, the DSB may authorize its Chairman to draw up the terms of reference of the panel in consultation with the parties to the dispute, subject to the provisions of paragraph 1. The terms of reference thus drawn up shall be circulated to all Members. If other than standard terms of reference are agreed upon, any Member may raise any point relating thereto in the DSB.

ARTICLE 8 COMPOSITION OF PANELS

1. Panels shall be composed of well-qualified governmental and/or non-governmental individuals, including persons who have served on or presented a case to a panel, served as a representative of a Member or of a contracting party to GATT 1947 or as a representative to the Council or Committee of any covered agreement or its predecessor agreement, or in the Secretariat, taught or published on international trade law or policy, or served as a senior trade policy official of a Member.
2. Panel members should be selected with a view to ensuring the independence of the members, a sufficiently diverse background and a wide spectrum of experience.
3. Citizens of Members whose governments are parties to the dispute or third parties as defined in paragraph 2 of Article 10 shall not serve on a panel concerned with that dispute, unless the parties to the dispute agree otherwise.
4. To assist in the selection of panelists, the Secretariat shall maintain an indicative list of governmental and non-governmental individuals possessing the qualifications outlined in paragraph 1, from which panelists may be drawn as appropriate. That list shall include the roster of non-governmental panelists established on 30 November 1984 (BISD 31S/9), and other rosters and indicative lists established under any of the covered agreements, and shall retain the names of persons on those rosters and indicative lists at the time of entry into force of the WTO Agreement. Members may periodically suggest names of governmental and non-governmental individuals for inclusion on the indicative list, providing relevant information on their knowledge of international trade and of the sectors or subject matter of the covered agreements, and those names shall be added to the list upon approval by the DSB. For each of the individuals on the list, the list shall indicate specific areas of experience or expertise of the individuals in the sectors or subject matter of the covered agreements.
5. Panels shall be composed of three panelists unless the parties to the dispute agree, within 10 days from the establishment of the panel, to a panel composed

of five panelists. Members shall be informed promptly of the composition of the panel.

6. The Secretariat shall propose nominations for the panel to the parties to the dispute. The parties to the dispute shall not oppose nominations except for compelling reasons.

7. If there is no agreement on the panelists within 20 days after the date of the establishment of a panel, at the request of either party, the Director-General, in consultation with the Chairman of the DSB and the Chairman of the relevant Council or Committee, shall determine the composition of the panel by appointing the panelists whom the Director-General considers most appropriate in accordance with any relevant special or additional rules or procedures of the covered agreement or covered agreements which are at issue in the dispute, after consulting with the parties to the dispute. The Chairman of the DSB shall inform the Members of the composition of the panel thus formed no later than 10 days after the date the Chairman receives such a request.

8. Members shall undertake, as a general rule, to permit their officials to serve as panelists.

9. Panelists shall serve in their individual capacities and not as government representatives, nor as representatives of any organization. Members shall therefore not give them instructions nor seek to influence them as individuals with regard to matters before a panel.

10. When a dispute is between a developing country Member and a developed country Member the panel shall, if the developing country Member so requests, include at least one panelist from a developing country Member.

11. Panelists' expenses, including travel and subsistence allowance, shall be met from the WTO budget in accordance with criteria to be adopted by the General Council, based on recommendations of the Committee on Budget, Finance and Administration.

ARTICLE 11 FUNCTION OF PANELS

The function of panels is to assist the DSB in discharging its responsibilities under this Understanding and the covered agreements. Accordingly, a panel should make an objective assessment of the matter before it, including an objective assessment of the facts of the case and the applicability of and conformity with the relevant covered agreements, and make such other findings as will assist the DSB in making the recommendations or in giving the rulings provided for in the covered agreements. Panels should consult regularly with the parties to the dispute and give them adequate opportunity to develop a mutually satisfactory solution.

ARTICLE 17 APPELLATE REVIEW

1. A standing Appellate Body shall be established by the DSB. The Appellate Body shall hear appeals from panel cases. It shall be composed of seven persons, three of whom shall serve on any one case. Persons serving on the Appellate Body shall serve in rotation. Such rotation shall be determined in the working procedures of the Appellate Body.

2. The DSB shall appoint persons to serve on the Appellate Body for a four-year term, and each person may be reappointed once. However, the terms of three

of the seven persons appointed immediately after the entry into force of the WTO Agreement shall expire at the end of two years, to be determined by lot. Vacancies shall be filled as they arise. A person appointed to replace a person whose term of office has not expired shall hold office for the remainder of the predecessor's term.

3. The Appellate Body shall comprise persons of recognized authority, with demonstrated expertise in law, international trade and the subject matter of the covered agreements generally. They shall be unaffiliated with any government. The Appellate Body membership shall be broadly representative of membership in the WTO. All persons serving on the Appellate Body shall be available at all times and on short notice, and shall stay abreast of dispute settlement activities and other relevant activities of the WTO. They shall not participate in the consideration of any disputes that would create a direct or indirect conflict of interest.

4. Only parties to the dispute, not third parties, may appeal a panel report. Third parties which have notified the DSB of a substantial interest in the matter pursuant to paragraph 2 of Article 10 may make written submissions to, and be given an opportunity to be heard by, the Appellate Body.

5. As a general rule, the proceedings shall not exceed 60 days from the date a party to the dispute formally notifies its decision to appeal to the date the Appellate Body circulates its report. In fixing its timetable the Appellate Body shall take into account the provisions of paragraph 9 of Article 4, if relevant. When the Appellate Body considers that it cannot provide its report within 60 days, it shall inform the DSB in writing of the reasons for the delay together with an estimate of the period within which it will submit its report. In no case shall the proceedings exceed 90 days.

6. An appeal shall be limited to issues of law covered in the panel report and legal interpretations developed by the panel.

7. The Appellate Body shall be provided with appropriate administrative and legal support as it requires.

8. The expenses of persons serving on the Appellate Body, including travel and subsistence allowance, shall be met from the WTO budget in accordance with criteria to be adopted by the General Council, based on recommendations of the Committee on Budget, Finance and Administration.

Procedures for Appellate Review

9. Working procedures shall be drawn up by the Appellate Body in consultation with the Chairman of the DSB and the Director-General, and communicated to the Members for their information.

10. The proceedings of the Appellate Body shall be confidential. The reports of the Appellate Body shall be drafted without the presence of the parties to the dispute and in the light of the information provided and the statements made.

11. Opinions expressed in the Appellate Body report by individuals serving on the Appellate Body shall be anonymous.

12. The Appellate Body shall address each of the issues raised in accordance with paragraph 6 during the appellate proceeding.

13. The Appellate Body may uphold, modify or reverse the legal findings and conclusions of the panel.

Adoption of Appellate Body Reports

14. An Appellate Body report shall be adopted by the DSB and unconditionally accepted by the parties to the dispute unless the DSB decides by consensus not to adopt the Appellate Body report within 30 days following its circulation to the Members. This adoption procedure is without prejudice to the right of Members to express their views on an Appellate Body report.

ARTICLE 23 STRENGTHENING OF THE MULTILATERAL SYSTEM

1. When Members seek the redress of a violation of obligations or other nullification or impairment of benefits under the covered agreements or an impediment to the attainment of any objective of the covered agreements, they shall have recourse to, and abide by, the rules and procedures of this Understanding.
2. In such cases, Members shall:
    (a) not make a determination to the effect that a violation has occurred, that benefits have been nullified or impaired or that the attainment of any objective of the covered agreements has been impeded, except through recourse to dispute settlement in accordance with the rules and procedures of this Understanding, and shall make any such determination consistent with the findings contained in the panel or Appellate Body report adopted by the DSB or an arbitration award rendered under this Understanding;
    (b) follow the procedures set forth in Article 21 to determine the reasonable period of time for the Member concerned to implement the recommendations and rulings; and
    (c) follow the procedures set forth in Article 22 to determine the level of suspension of concessions or other obligations and obtain DSB authorization in accordance with those procedures before suspending concessions or other obligations under the covered agreements in response to the failure of the Member concerned to implement the recommendations and rulings within that reasonable period of time.

ARTICLE 27 RESPONSIBILITIES OF THE SECRETARIAT

1. The Secretariat shall have the responsibility of assisting panels, especially on the legal, historical and procedural aspects of the matters dealt with, and of providing secretarial and technical support.
2. While the Secretariat assists Members in respect of dispute settlement at their request, there may also be a need to provide additional legal advice and assistance in respect of dispute settlement to developing country Members. To this end, the Secretariat shall make available a qualified legal expert from the WTO technical cooperation services to any developing country Member which so requests. This expert shall assist the developing country Member in a manner ensuring the continued impartiality of the Secretariat.

3. The Secretariat shall conduct special training courses for interested Members concerning these dispute settlement procedures and practices so as to enable Members' experts to be better informed in this regard.

Annex 2: section 3 of the VCLT, interpretation of treaties

ARTICLE 31 GENERAL RULE OF INTERPRETATION

1. A treaty shall be interpreted in good faith in accordance with the ordinary meaning to be given to the terms of the treaty in their context and in the light of its object and purpose.
2. The context for the purpose of the interpretation of a treaty shall comprise, in addition to the text, including its preamble and annexes: (a) any agreement relating to the treaty which was made between all the parties in connection with the conclusion of the treaty; (b) any instrument which was made by one or more parties in connection with the conclusion of the treaty and accepted by the other parties as an instrument related to the treaty.
3. There shall be taken into account, together with the context:
   (a) any subsequent agreement between the parties regarding the interpretation of the treaty or the application of its provisions;
   (b) any subsequent practice in the application of the treaty which establishes the agreement of the parties regarding its interpretation;
   (c) any relevant rules of international law applicable in the relations between the parties.
4. A special meaning shall be given to a term if it is established that the parties so intended.

ARTICLE 32 SUPPLEMENTARY MEANS OF INTERPRETATION

Recourse may be had to supplementary means of interpretation, including the preparatory work of the treaty and the circumstances of its conclusion, in order to confirm the meaning resulting from the application of article 31, or to determine the meaning when the interpretation according to article 31:
(a) leaves the meaning ambiguous or obscure; or
(b) leads to a result which is manifestly absurd or unreasonable.

ARTICLE 33 INTERPRETATION OF TREATIES AUTHENTICATED IN TWO OR MORE LANGUAGES

1. When a treaty has been authenticated in two or more languages, the text is equally authoritative in each language, unless the treaty provides or the parties agree that, in case of divergence, a particular text shall prevail.
2. A version of the treaty in a language other than one of those in which the text was authenticated shall be considered an authentic text only if the treaty so provides or the parties so agree.
3. The terms of the treaty are presumed to have the same meaning in each authentic text.
4. Except where a particular text prevails in accordance with paragraph 1, when a comparison of the authentic texts discloses a difference of meaning which the application of articles 31 and 32 does not remove, the meaning which best reconciles the texts, having regard to the object and purpose of the treaty, shall be adopted.

References

Abi-Saab, Georges. 2010. The Appellate Body and Treaty Interpretation. pp. 99–109 in Malgosia Fitzmaurice, Olufemi Elias and Panos Merkouris (eds.). Treaty Interpretation and the Vienna Convention on the Law of Treaties: 30 Years On, Brill Publishers: Leiden, the Netherlands.

Algero, Mary Garvey. 2005. The Sources of Law and the Value of Precedent: A Comparative and Empirical Study of a Civil Law State in a Common Law Nation, Louisiana Law Review, 65: 775–822.

Alter, Karen J. 2008. Agents or Trustees? International Courts in their Political Context, European Journal of International Relations, 14: 33–63.

Alvarez-Jimenez, Alberto. 2011. Identification of Customary International Law in the International Court of Justice's Jurisprudence, 2000–2009, The International and Comparative Law Quarterly, 60: 681–712.

Antràs, Pol. 2014. Grossman-Hart (1986) Goes Global: Incomplete Contracts, Property Rights, and the International Organization of Production, Journal of Law, Economics, and Organization, 30: 118–75.

Arangio-Ruiz, Gaetano. 1992. Fourth Report on State Responsibility, ILC Yearbook, Vol. II, Part One, United Nations: New York City, New York.

Barkow, Rachel. 2002. More Supreme Court? The Fall of the Political Question Doctrine, and the Rise of Judicial Supremacy, Columbia Law Review, 102: 237–336.

Bartels, Lorand. 2001. Applicable Law in WTO Dispute Settlement Proceedings, Journal of World Trade, 35: 499–519.

Benedek, Wolfgang. 1990. Das GATT aus Völkerrechtlicher Sicht, Springer Verlag: Heidelberg.

Benvenisti, Eyal. 2004. Customary International Law as Judicial Tool for Promoting Judicial Efficiency, pp. 85–116 in Eyal Benvenisti and Moshe Hirsch (eds.). The Impact of International Law on International Cooperation, Cambridge University Press: Cambridge, United Kingdom.

Benvenisti, Eyal, and George W. Downs. 2007. The Empire's New Clothes: Political Economy and the Fragmentation of International Law, Stanford Law Review, 60: 595–631.

Bernheim, B. Douglas and Michael D. Whinston. 1986. Common Agency, Econometrica, 54: 923–42.

Beviglia-Zampetti, Americo, Patrick Low and Petros C. Mavroidis. 2022. Consensus Decision-Making and Legislative Inertia in the WTO: Can International Law Help? Journal of World Trade, 56: 1–26.

Bingham, Tom. 2011. The Rule of Law, Penguin Books: London, United Kingdom.

Brown, Christopher. 1996. A Comparative and Critical Assessment of Estoppel in International Law, University of Miami Law Review, 50: 369–412.

Busch, Marc L. and Krzysztof J. Pelc. 2010. The Politics of Judicial Economy at the World Trade Organization, International Organization, 64: 257–79.

Butler, Graham. 2018. In Search of the Political Question Doctrine in EU Law, Legal Issues of Economic Integration, 45: 329–54.

Charwat, Nicola. 2016. Who Participates As Amicus Curiae in World Trade Organisation Dispute Settlement and Why? New Zealand Universities Law Review, 27: 337–64 (available at SSRN: https://ssrn.com/abstract=3021553).

Cheng, Bin. 1953. General Principles of Law Applied by International Courts and Tribunals, Stevens & Sons, Ltd.: London, United Kingdom.

Cook, Graham. 2015. A Digest of WTO Jurisprudence on Public International Law Concepts and Principles, Cambridge University Press: Cambridge, United Kingdom.

Davey, William J. 2003. Has the WTO Dispute Settlement Exceeded its Authority? A Consideration of Deference Shown by the System to Member Government Decisions and its Use of Issue-Avoidance Techniques, pp. 43–80 in Thomas Cottier, Petros C. Mavroidis and Patrick Blatter (eds.). The Role of the Judge in International Trade Regulation, Experience and Lessons for the WTO, University of Michigan Press: Ann Arbor, Michigan.

Davey, William J. 2015. The First Years of WTO Dispute Settlement: Dealing with Controversy and Building Confidence, pp. 353–62 in Gabrielle Marceau (ed.). A History of Law and Lawyers in the GATT/WTO, Cambridge University Press & the WTO: Geneva, Switzerland.

Denning, Alfred Thompson. 2005. The Discipline of Law, Oxford University Press: Oxford, United Kingdom.

Distefano, Giovanni. 2011. L'interprétation évolutive de la norme internationale, Revue générale de droit international public, 115: 373–96.

Dworkin, Ronald. 1977. Taking Rights Seriously, Harvard University Press: Cambridge, Massachusetts.

Easterbrook, Frank H. 1984. The Limits of Antitrust, Texas Law Review, 63: 1–40.

Ehlermann, Claus-Dieter. 2002. Six Years on the Bench of the "World Trade Court": Some Personal Experiences as a Member of the Appellate Body of the World Trade Organization, Journal of World Trade, 36: 605–39.

Ehring, Lothar. 2008. Public Access to Dispute Settlement Hearings in the World Trade Organization, Journal of International Economic Law, 11: 1021–34.

Fiorini, Matteo, Bernard M. Hoekman, Petros C. Mavroidis, Maarja Saluste and Robert Wolfe. 2020. WTO Dispute Settlement and the Appellate Body Crisis: Insider Perceptions and Members' Revealed Preferences, Journal of World Trade, 54: 667–98.

Fitzmaurice, Gerald. 1974. The Problem of *Non Liquet*: Prolegomena to a Restatement, pp. 89–112 in Mélanges offerts a Charles Rousseau: La Communauté Internationale, Pédone: Paris, France.

Friedmann, Wolfgang. 1966. Limits of the Judicial Law-Making and Prospective Overruling, Modern Law Review, 29: 593–607.

Fuller, Lon. 1969. The Anatomy of Law, Praeger Publishing: New York City, New York.

Gailmard, Sean. 2009. Multiple Principals and Oversight of Bureaucratic Policy-Making, Journal of Theoretical Politics, 21: 161–86.

Grossman, Gene M. and Petros C. Mavroidis. 2007. Recurring Misunderstanding of Non-Recurring Subsidies, US–Certain EC Products, pp. 381–90 in Henrik Horn and Petros C. Mavroidis (eds.). The WTO Case Law, The American Law Institute Reporters' Studies, Cambridge University Press: Cambridge, United Kingdom.

Grossman, Sanford J. and Oliver D. Hart. 1986. The Costs and Benefits of Ownership: A Theory of Vertical and Lateral Integration, Journal of Political Economy, 94: 691–719.

Haass, Richard N. 2017. A World in Disarray, Penguin Books: New York City, New York.

Hart, H.L.A. 1961. The Concept of Law, Oxford University Press: Oxford, United Kingdom.

Hart, Nina M. and Brandon J. Murrill. 2021. The World Trade Organization's (WTO's) Appellate Body: Key Disputes and Controversies, Congressional Research Service, R46852: Washington D.C.

Henkin, Louis. 1976. Is There a Political Question Doctrine? Yale Law Journal, 85: 597–625.

Higgins, Rosalyn. 1994. Problems and Process: International Law and How We Use It, Clarendon Press: Oxford, United Kingdom.

Holmes, Oliver Wendell. 1991. The Common Law (revised edition), Dover Publications: Mineola, New York.

Horn, Henrik, Giovanni Maggi and Robert W. Staiger. 2010. Trade Agreements as Endogenously Incomplete Contracts, American Economic Review, 100: 394–419.

Horn, Henrik and Petros C. Mavroidis. 2009. Burden of Proof in Environmental Disputes in the WTO: Legal Aspects, European Energy and Environmental Law Review, 18: 112–40.

Hovenkamp, Herbert. 2022. Antitrust Error Costs, available at https://scholarship.law .upenn.edu/faculty_scholarship/2742/.

Hudec, Robert E. 1993. Enforcing International Trade Law: The Evolution of the Modern GATT Legal System, Butterworth: Oxford, United Kingdom.

Hynning, Christopher J. 1956. Sources of International Law, Chicago-Kent Law Review, 34: 116–35.

Jackson, John H. 1969. World Trade and the Law of the GATT, Bobbs-Merrill: Indianapolis, Indiana.

Jimenez de Arréchaga, Eduardo. 1978. International Law in the Past Third of the Century, Recueil des Cours, 159, Brill Academic Publishers: the Hague, the Netherlands.

Kahneman, Daniel, Olivier Sibony and Cass R. Sunstein. 2021. Noise, a Flaw in Human Judgment, Little Brown Spark: New York, Boston, London.

Kaplow, Louis. 1992. Rules Versus Standards: an Economic Analysis, Duke Law Journal, 42: 557–629.

Kaplow, Louis. 2012. Burden of Proof, Yale Law Journal, 121: 738–839.

Kearney, Joseph D. and Thomas W. Merrill. 2000. The Influence of Amicus Curiae Briefs on the Supreme Court, University of Pennsylvania Law Review, 148: 743–98.

Khalil, Fahad, David Martimort and Bruno Parigi. 2007. Monitoring a Common Agent: Implications for Financial Contracting, Journal of Economic Theory, 135: 35–67.

Koremenos, Barbara. 2007. If Only Half of International Agreements Have Dispute Resolution Provisions, Which Half Needs Explaining? Journal of Legal Studies, 36: 189–211.

Kuijper, Pieter Jan. 1994. The Law of GATT as a Special Field of International Law: Ignorance, Further Refinement or Self-Contained System of International Law? Netherlands Yearbook of International Law, 25: 227–57.

Lang, Andrew and Joanne Scott. 2009. The Hidden World of WTO Governance, European Journal of International Law, 20: 575–614.

Lauterpacht, Hersch. 1927. Private Law Sources and Analogies in International Law, Longmans, Green & Co.: New York City, New York.

Lauterpacht, Hersch. 1958. Some Observations on the Prohibition of 'Non Liquet' and the Completeness of the Law, pp. 196–221 in Frederik M. van Asbeck (ed.).

Symbolae Verzijl: Présentées au Prof J.H.W. Verzijl, à l'occasion de son LXXième anniversaire, Martinus Nijhoff: the Hague, the Netherlands.

Marceau, Gabrielle. 2002. WTO Dispute Settlement and Human Rights, European Journal of International Law, 13: 753–814.

Marceau, Gabrielle (ed.). 2015. A History of Law and Lawyers in the GATT/WTO, Cambridge University Press & the WTO: Geneva, Switzerland.

Mascini, Peter and Nina L. Holvast. 2020. Explaining Judicial Assistants' Influence on Adjudication with Principal–Agent Theory and Contextual Factors. International Journal for Court Administration, 11: 5–23.

Mattoo, Aaditya, Nadia Rocha and Michele Ruta (eds.). 2020. Handbook of Deep Trade Agreements, The World Bank Group: Washington, D.C.

Mavroidis, Petros C. 1991. Das GATT als Self-Contained Régime, Recht der Internationalen Wirtschaft, 6: 497–501.

Mavroidis, Petros C. 2002. Amicus Curiae Briefs Before the WTO: Much Ado About Nothing, pp. 317–29 in Armin von Bogdandy, Petros C. Mavroidis and Yves Meny (eds.). European Integration and International Co-ordination, Studies in Trans-national Economic Law in Honour of Claus-Dieter Ehlermann, Kluwer: Leiden, the Netherlands.

Mavroidis, Petros C. 2008. No Outsourcing of Law? WTO Law as Practiced by WTO Courts, American Journal of International Law, 102: 421–74.

Mavroidis, Petros C. 2016. The Regulation of International Trade, volume 2, MIT Press: Cambridge, Massachusetts.

Mavroidis, Petros C. 2019. Last Mile for Tuna (to a Safe Harbour): What is the TBT Agreement All About? European Journal of International Law, 30: 279–301.

Mavroidis, Petros C. 2022. The WTO Dispute Settlement System, How, Why, and Where? Edward Elgar Publishing: Northampton, Massachusetts, Cheltenham, United Kingdom.

Mavroidis, Petros C. and André Sapir. 2021. China and the WTO, Why Multilateralism Matters, Princeton University Press: Princeton, New Jersey.

McDougall, Robert. 2018. The Crisis in WTO Dispute Settlement: Fixing Birth Defects to Restore Balance, Journal of World Trade, 52: 867–96.

Mortenson, Julian Davis. 2013. The Travaux of Travaux: Is the Vienna Convention Hostile to Drafting History? American Journal of International Law, 107: 780–822.

Ortino, Federico. 2009. The Impact of Amicus Curiae Briefs in the Settlement of Trade and Investment Disputes, pp. 301–16 in K. Meessen, M. Bungenber and A. Puttler (eds.). Economic Law as an Economic Good: Its Rule Function and its Tool Function in the Competition of Systems, European Law Publishers: Munich, Germany.

Orwell, George. 1946. Politics and the English Language, Penguin: London, United Kingdom.

Palmeter, N. David. 1998. The WTO Appellate Body Needs Remand Authority, Journal of World Trade, 32: 41–4.

Palmeter, N. David and Petros C. Mavroidis. 1998. The WTO Legal System: Sources of Law, American Journal of International Law, 92: 398–413.

Palmeter, N. David, Petros C. Mavroidis and Niall Meagher. 2022. Dispute Settlement in the World Trade Organization, Practice and Procedure, 3rd Edition, Cambridge University Press: Cambridge, United Kingdom.

Pauwelyn, Joost. 2003. Conflict of Norms in Public International Law, Oxford University Press: Oxford, United Kingdom.

Pound, Roscoe. 1946. Sources and Forms of Law, Notre Dame Lawyer, A Quarterly Law Review, XXI: 247–314.

Prusa, Thomas J. and Edwin Vermulst. 2009. A One-Two Punch on Zeroing: U.S.–Zeroing (EC) and U.S.–Zeroing (Japan), World Trade Review, 8: 187–241.

Rehnquist, William H. 1957. Who Writes Decisions of the Supreme Court? U.S. News & World Report, December 13, 74.

Reisman, W. Michael. 1969. International Non-Liquet, Recrudescence and Transformation, The International Lawyer, 4: 770–86.

Remy Nash, Jonathan and Rafael I. Pardo. 2013. Re-thinking the Principal–Agent Theory of Judging, Iowa Law Review, 99: 331–62.

Riphagen, Willem. 1982. Third Report on State Responsibility, International Law Commission (ILC) Yearbook, Vol. II, Part One, United Nations: New York City, New York.

Rosenne, Shabtai. 1965. The Law and Practice of the International Court, Martinus Nijhoff Publishers: Dordrecht, the Netherlands.

Sacerdoti, Giorgio. 2020. The Authority of "Precedent" in International Adjudication: The Contentious Case of the WTO's Appellate Practice, The Law and Practice of International Courts and Tribunals, 19: 497–514.

Scalia, Antonin. 1997. A Matter of Interpretation, Federal Courts and the Law, Princeton University Press: Princeton, New Jersey.

Simma, Bruno. 1985. Self-Contained Regimes, Netherlands Yearbook of International Law, 16: 111–36.

Simma, Bruno and Dirk Pulkowski. 2006. Of Planets and the Universe: Self-contained Regimes in International Law, European Journal of International Law, 17: 483–529.

Steinberg, Richard H. 2002. In the Shadow of Law or Power? Consensus-Based Bargaining and Outcomes in the GATT/WTO, International Organization, 56: 339–74.

Stith, Kate and José A. Cabranes. 1998. Fear of Judging, The University of Chicago Press: Chicago, Illinois.

Stone, Julius. 1954. Lega Controls of International Conflict, Stevens and Sons: London, United Kingdom.

Sunstein, Cass R. 2001. One Case at a Time, Harvard University Press: Cambridge, Massachusetts.

Sykes, Alan O. 2006. The WTO Agreement on Safeguards: A Commentary, Oxford University Press: New York City, New York.

Thirlway, Hugh. 2019. The Sources of International Law, 2nd edition, Oxford University Press: Oxford, United Kingdom.

Trachtman, Joel. 1999. The Domain of WTO Dispute Resolution, Harvard International Law Journal, 40: 333–80.

Trachtman, Joel. 2004. Conflict of Norms in Public International Law: How WTO Law Relates to Other Rules of International Law, American Journal of International Law, 98: 855–902.

USTR. 2020. Report on the Functioning of the Appellate Body of the World Trade Organization, USTR (United States Trade representative): Washington D.C., available at https://ustr.gov/sites/default/files/enforcement/DS/USTR.Appellate.Body.Rpt.Feb2020.pdf.

Van Damme, Isabelle. 2009. Treaty Interpretation by the WTO Appellate Body, Oxford University Press: Oxford, United Kingdom.

Ventouratou, Anna. 2021. The Law on State Responsibility and the World Trade Organization, The Journal of World Investment & Trade, 22: 759–803.

Verdross, Alfred. 1966. Jus Dispositivum and Jus Cogens in International Law, American Journal of International Law, 60: 55–63.

Villiger, Mark E. 2008. Commentary on the 1969 Vienna Convention on the Law of Treaties, Brill Publishing: Leiden, the Netherlands.

Virally, Michel. 1983. Review Essay: Good Faith in Public International Law, American Journal of International Law, 77: 130–34.

Weil, Prosper. 1998. The Court Cannot Conclude Definitively, Non Liquet Revisited, Columbia Journal of Transnational Law, 36: 109–19.

Wetzel, Ralph Günther and Dietrich Rauschning. 1978. The Vienna Convention on the Law of Treaties: Travaux Preparatoires, Metzner Verlag: Frankfurt am Main, Germany.

Wittgenstein, Ludwig. 1953. Philosophical Investigations, Blackwell Publishing: Oxford, United Kingdom.

Wolfe, Robert. 2009. The Single Undertaking as Negotiating Technique and Constitutive Metaphor, Journal of International Economic Law, 12: 835–58.

Zoller, Elizabeth. 1977. La Bonne Foi en Droit International, Pedone: Paris, France.

Index

Printed and bound by CPI Group (UK) Ltd, Croydon, CR0 4YY

09/06/2025